KARL MANNHEIM

KEY SOCIOLOGISTS
Series Editor: Peter Hamilton
The Open University

KEY SOCIOLOGISTS

Series Editor: PETER HAMILTON
The Open University, Milton Keynes

This series will present concise and readable texts covering the work, life and influence of many of the most important sociologists, and sociologically-relevant thinkers, from the birth of the discipline to the present day. Aimed primarily at the undergraduate, the books will also be useful to pre-university students and others who are interested in the main ideas of sociology's major thinkers.

MARX and Marxism
PETER WORSLEY, Professor of Sociology, University of Manchester

MAX WEBER
FRANK PARKIN, Tutor in Politics and Fellow of Magdalen College, Oxford

EMILE DURKHEIM
KENNETH THOMPSON, Reader in Sociology, Faculty of Social Sciences, The Open University, Milton Keynes

TALCOTT PARSONS
PETER HAMILTON, The Open University, Milton Keynes

SIGMUND FREUD
ROBERT BOCOCK, The Open University, Milton Keynes

C. WRIGHT MILLS
J. E. T. ELDRIDGE, Department of Sociology, University of Glasgow

THE FRANKFURT SCHOOL
TOM BOTTOMORE, Professor of Sociology, University of Sussex

GEORG SIMMEL
DAVID FRISBY, Department of Sociology, The University, Glasgow

KARL MANNHEIM
DAVID KETTLER, Professor of Political Studies, Trent University, Ontario, Canada
VOLKER MEJA, Associate Professor of Sociology, Memorial University of Newfoundland, and
NICO STEHR, Professor of Sociology, University of Alberta

KARL MANNHEIM

DAVID KETTLER
Professor of Political Studies
Trent University, Ontario, Canada
VOLKER MEJA
Associate Professor of Sociology
Memorial University of Newfoundland
NICO STEHR
Professor of Sociology
University of Alberta, Canada

ELLIS HORWOOD LIMITED
Publishers · Chichester

TAVISTOCK PUBLICATIONS
London and New York

First published in 1984
ELLIS HORWOOD LIMITED
Market Cross House, Cooper Street
Chichester, Sussex, PO19 1EB, England
and

TAVISTOCK PUBLICATIONS LIMITED
11 New Fetter Lane, London EC4P 4EE

Published in the USA by
TAVISTOCK PUBLICATIONS
and ELLIS HORWOOD LIMITED
in association with METHUEN INC.
733 Third Avenue, New York, NY 10017

British Library Cataloguing in Publication Data
Kettler, David
Karl Mannheim. – (Key sociologists)
1. Mannheim, Karl 2. Knowledge, Sociology of
I. Title II. Meja, Volker III. Stehr, Nico IV. Series
306'.42   BD175.M323
Library of Congress Card No. 84-552

ISBN 0-85312-687-9 (Ellis Horwood Ltd. – Library Edn.)
ISBN 0-85312-688-7 (Ellis Horwood Ltd. – Student Edn.)

Printed in Great Britain by R.J. Acford, Chichester.

Table of Contents

Editor's Foreword   7

Acknowledgements   10

Introduction   11

Chapter 1
Politics as a Science   14

Chapter 2
The Ways of Knowledge   33

Chapter 3
Diagnostic Sociology   81

Chapter 4
Towards a Rational Society?   129

Conclusion: Sociology as a Vocation   151

Suggestions for Further Reading   164

Index   166

DAVID KETTLER has been Professor of Political Studies at Trent University, Ontario, Canada, since 1971. He was formerly Professor of Political Science at Ohio State University. He belongs to several important societies, both in Europe and America, and has written or edited several other books, two of which were published in both German and English.

VOLKER MEJA became Associate Professor at the Memorial University of Newfoundland in 1976, having joined the University in 1972 as Assistant Professor. He was previously Lecturer in Sociology at the Southeastern Massachusetts University. He has edited several books, and is Editor of the *Newsletter of the International Society for the Sociology of Knowledge.*

NICO STEHR first joined the University of Alberta in Canada in 1970, as Assistant Professor. He was appointed Associate Professor in 1974, and became Professor in 1978. He has also been a Visiting Professor at Zurich University (Switzerland), Konstanz University (West Germany) and the University of Calgary (Canada). He, too, is the co-editor of several books, and Editor of the *Canadian Journal of Sociology.*

Editor's Foreword

Karl Mannheim is probably best known for his work *Ideology and Utopia*, which has done so much to establish the sociology of knowledge as a distinctive concern within sociological theory. However, his work as an exiled intellectual in Britain from 1933 to his death in 1947 also did much to establish sociology in that country as a respectable academic discipline rather than a form of political theory, social philosophy or mere fact-gathering. That his role in the renaissance of British sociology should have come about partly as a result of his fundamental misunderstanding of its history and of the intellectual milieux in which it arose is only one of the many paradoxes that characterized the life of this twice-exiled and somewhat lonely figure of European sociology. David Kettler, Volker Meja and Nico Stehr have succeeded in encompassing the surprising scope and richness of Mannheim's sociology in this book, which is sure to become the standard introduction to this most intriguing and complex of sociologists. The authors have delved deeply in the archives to bring out many hitherto unknown materials relating to Mannheim's life and work, which are reflected in this major reassessment of his contribution to modern sociology.

Mannheim's sociology always allotted a central role to the socially aware intellectual as the carrier of knowledge about how society works. Yet his conception of a relatively 'free-floating' stratum of thinkers relatively unconnected to any single social class was an attempt to marry liberalism and rationalism to the ideal of a science of politics which was ultimately unrealizable. Nonetheless his concern to find a formulation for sociological thinking at a mid-point between sociology and philosophy led to the emergence of a distinctive sociology of knowledge, which Mannheim hoped would form one element in a mediation of *liberal* and *conservative* ideologies. He was the first sociologist to subject political ideologies to a thoroughgoing sociological analysis, and his work has for long formed a starting point for the study of ideological systems. It is indeed tempting to apply the specialism he was so influential in establishing to the ideas which Mannheim created. Thus, a sociology of knowledge applied to Mannheim's principal works would emphasize his upbringing and education as a German-speaking Jew in the last years of the Austro-Hungarian empire: his brief involvement in the liberal and Soviet regimes which ruled Hungary in 1918–19, and his friendship with Bela Kun's Minister of Culture, Georg Lukács; subsequent exile in Weimar Germany until the advent of the Nazi state in 1933, when because he was a Jew he lost his chair in sociology at the University of Frankfurt; and finally a further very difficult period of exile in Britain until his death in 1947, during which he exemplified the refugee European scholar, painfully aware of the gulf between his own speculative and philosophically sophisticated sociology which was culturally rooted in Germanic intellectual life, and the sturdy pragmatism of his hosts. Whilst he could have gone to America (where so many of his German and central European colleagues found themselves during the Nazi period) Mannheim stayed in Britain, determined to play a part in the rebuilding of sociology along more theoretically advanced lines. Having developed a sort of 'sociology of planning', Mannheim saw Britain as the ideal location for its propagation. It is sad that the handicaps of his own cultural background blinded him to the fact that the issues he so energetically promoted as novelties were in fact longstanding problems well known to English sociology. Perhaps he mistook the primitive and almost non-existent establishment of sociology within British higher education as evidence of theoretical backwardness, ignoring the fact that sociology had been developed in Britain since at least the time of Spencer in the nineteenth century. Indeed, one of the most interesting sections of this fascinating book is Kettler, Meja and Stehr's account of Mannheim's period in Britain. Despite his misconceptions about the role and status of British sociology, the contact with Mannheim's ideas was clearly important in influencing certain trends in its later development. His part in the establishment of the Routledge & Kegan Paul International Library of Sociology and Social Reconstruction shortly before his death led to a publishing venture which has become part of the institutional structure of post-war British sociology. And perhaps Mannheim did help to bridge the gulf between continental social theory of the type created by Max Weber, Werner Sombart, the Frankfurt School theorists and others, and the more pragmatic and 'middle-range' theoretical concerns of the British sociologists.

Throughout his life Mannheim was searching for ways of founding a science of politics which would harness the forces of irrationality and permit the creation of a rational political order. It is in tracing out how this essentially moral concern suffuses the whole of Mannheim's sociological work that David Kettler, Volker Meja and Nico Stehr help us to see the importance of his role as a mediator between several realms – between politics and reason, between philosophy and sociology, and between European and Anglo-Saxon modes of intellectual thought. As a marginal 'outsider' Mannheim played the role well; yet in an important sense he also stands in a mediatory relationship to the sociological concerns of the founders of modern sociology such as Weber, and to the professionalization of sociology since the 1940s which has finally brought about the emergence of a socially aware and 'free-floating' intelligentsia. But it is ironic to note that this has not made politics more scientific and rational, as Mannheim hoped, but deepened the conflict between what he called ideologies and utopias.

Peter Hamilton

Acknowledgements

We are grateful for the assistance of Judith Adler, Charles Cooper, Joseph Gabel, Éva Gábor, Johan Goudsblom, Peter Hamilton, Gianfranco Poggi, Henk Woldring, Kurt H. Wolff, and Victor Zaslavsky. We are also indebted to our departments at the Memorial University of Newfoundland, Trent University, and the University of Alberta, as well as to the Bard College Center, and the Netherlands Institute for Advanced Study. Work on this book was financially supported by the Social Sciences and Humanities Research Council (Ottawa), Trent University, and the Memorial University of Newfoundland.

Introduction

Karl Mannheim was born in Budapest in 1893. He earned a degree in philosophy at the university there, with a thesis on the structure of epistemology. In 1919, after the successive collapses of the two post-war revolutionary regimes in Hungary, Mannheim settled in Germany. He had already spent one of his student years there, attending Simmel's lectures in cultural philosophy and sociology, and now established himself as a private scholar in Heidelberg. He attended Alfred Weber's seminars and worked closely with Emil Lederer, and these two sociologists sponsored his successful *Habilitation* as *Privatdozent*, on the strength of a sociological study of German conservatism in the nineteenth century. He gave seminars for several years in Heidelberg, until he was called, after several noted publications and a brilliant debut at the German Sociological Congress in 1928, to succeed Franz Oppenheimer as Professor of Sociology at Frankfurt. As a recently naturalized citizen and Jew, he was suspended from his position by one of the first National Socialist enactments, in April of 1933. Invited to London by Harold Laski, on behalf of English scholars eager to rescue outstanding university people victimized by the Nazis, he spent the next ten years as lecturer at the London School of Economics. In the middle of the war, then, he was appointed to the new professorship in the sociology of education at the University of London. He died in 1947 at the age of 53.

During this stressful and brief intellectual career, Mannheim produced much work highly regarded by his contemporaries, and he twice published major books which set the agenda for extensive discussions within and among several disciplines. It is still impossible to think critically about the sociology of knowledge without reflecting on *Ideology and Utopia*. And the continuing debates about planning recurrently return to *Man and Society in an Age of Reconstruction*. These books have had careers in several countries, at different times. In its German original, *Ideology and Utopia* attracted fascinated reviews from Hannah Arendt, Max Horkheimer, Herbert Marcuse, Paul Tillich, and other outstanding representatives of the younger intellectual generation. In its English version, it has had an extraordinary career in the United States, after an initial reception which helped to begin the careers of Robert K. Merton and C. Wright Mills. The work on crisis, reconstruction, and planning began as a German-language reflection on the German disaster, addressed primarily to emigrants, but played a major part in the English wartime debate on planning, intrigued John Dewey and Louis Mumford, as well as setting a major challenge to Karl R. Popper, Friedrich Hayek, Robert A. Dahl and Charles E. Lindblom, and introduced the post-war generation to political sociology. Major collections of additional works by Mannheim have been published in English and German during each of the last four decades, including posthumous introduction of works which Mannheim himself never published.

Yet Mannheim's position as a major sociological thinker is by no means secure. His philosophical interests and speculative methods make him somewhat suspect to many empirical sociologists; and his earnest search for scientific ways of disciplining his enquiries put off anti-positivists. It is only as these simplistic oppositions lose plausibility that the undeniable presence of Mannheim at the starting points for the most compelling questions can be acknowledged, and the riddles of his achievements and failings can be recognized as bearing directly on those of the present.

There are useful ways of dealing with his contributions to various specialized sub-disciplines, such as the study of political ideologies, the sociology of other intellectual and cultural forms, the sociology of organization, planning, political sociology, sociology of education, and so on. The way chosen for the interpretative essay presented here tries, instead, to clarify the design which brought him to all these matters. The suggestion of a design is not meant to indicate that there is some grand unified theory to be found or an elegant dialectical progression through his works. There is, rather, a search and a complex sensibility and a distinctive openness to hard findings about the social world. The story of Mannheim is the story of someone working at social theorizing. He writes essays but aspires to synthesis and system; he wants to dig empirically and dig deep but he feels called to give concrete advice; he cannot stop reflecting on the place and role of intellectuals but he takes as a model the knowledge of the practical actor who commands a situation.

Political thinking and thinking about politics play a part in his thinking, even when he seems to be putting them aside. His preoccupation with ideologies derives from the conviction that they are decisive to the most fascinating and determinative processes in human life, and his own findings must somehow bear on the matters that ideologies are about and not only what they do in society. In consequence, this book begins with an interpretation of Mannheim's political interest. Since that interest will prove to pose problems about the nature of knowledge, the opening is by no means designed to unveil and expose discrediting compulsions. Attention shifts, rather, to his explorations of the knowledge required for the rational conduct of human life and to his determination that sociological study bears decisively upon its formation. Then comes the crisis that undermines the plausibility of the intellectual strategy Mannheim has been projecting, and the search for alternatives. This requires somewhat more attention to his actual situation than did the earlier themes, and the closing chapter returns to the questions about his overall design and about the significance of the way chosen to study it.

Mannheim belongs to a cultural generation and style that values hints and allusions and multiple meanings, even while it acknowledges the authority of rigorous method and the power of firm evidence. To trace his thinking requires some patience and a certain tolerance for essayistic experimentation. There is always time for harsh questions later. Mannheim was a great admirer of sociologists: he was intrigued by what they did even when he still doubted their philosophical sophistication. This curiosity and respect led him to probe into the discipline again and again, even before he thought it would be his own. In the end, he determined he had to try it. Sociology was changed by this.

1

Politics as a Science

MANNHEIM AND LIBERAL POLITICAL THOUGHT

Karl Mannheim often commented on the social condition of the outsider, who stands on the margin of an integrated social field, or on the boundary between two or more. No condition could have been more familiar to him. While the position of a Jewish student and young intellectual in the Budapest of 1910 may have been 'marginal' only when viewed from the nationalist perspective easy enough for this circle to dismiss, he twice in his life underwent the experience of exile and twice had to find a voice and a language appropriate to a newcomer. He left Hungary in 1919, after the failures of the progressive liberal and Soviet regimes; and he fled Germany for England in 1933, after the National Socialist decree deprived him of the Frankfurt professorship which he had only recently gained.

But it was not only the force of circumstances which brought him repeatedly to the boundary. Already as a young man in Budapest he had chosen an intellectual place for himself between proponents of reform based on social science, led by Oscar Jászi, and advocates of cultural renovation grounded on an essentially aesthetic philosophy, under George Lukács. And later, during his German academic career, he long prided himself on standing between sociology and philosophy, as well as between the exciting world of intellectuals' criticisms and the exacting world of academic rigour.[1] Mannheim's English writings include reflections on the role of the refugee, and on his special mission as a mediator between European and Anglo-Saxon intellectual modes; and he aimed his work at creating conjunctions between sociology and education, between the preoccupations of practical reformers and those of the university.[2]

Mannheim was by no means content simply to enjoy the ironic distance and special insights which the boundary condition is sometimes thought to provide. He believed that it also creates a unique opportunity to mediate between antithetical forces and to work for syntheses, and, indeed, that it implies a mission to do so. In his accounts of the sociology of knowledge, the enquiry for which he is best known, he emphasizes that the very possibility of such an approach to ideas and culture depends on the existence of a social stratum whose members have lived in diverse cultural and social settings and are now situated where they can experience that diversity.[3] But the point of their intellectual labours is not to be, according to Mannheim, an impressionistic relish of variety, but rather a restoration of a common spirit and joint direction to the society as a whole.

This very preoccupation with bridging mutually alien worlds, overcoming conflicts, and cultivating comprehensive unities gives a certain political cast to his thought, or at least provides one source of his interest in political thinking. Mannheim's two best-known works both treat materials of primary interest to political writers. In *Ideology and Utopia*, he subjects complexes of political ideas to sociological interpretation, and in *Man and Society in an Age of Reconstruction* he proposes a design for reorganizing the social order so as to overcome the crisis afflicting public life. In both books, however, he disregards many of the primary concepts of political discourse and many of the issues discussed in political theory. In these writings, questions of rational public policy displace questions of legitimate authority, justice, citizenship, or the best constitution. In Mannheim's work we find ideology and sociology instead of political theory, and, especially in his later writings,"elites' instead of governors, techniques of social control instead of law, command or coercion, questions of integration and coordination instead of power and resistance. Nevertheless, it is justified to see Karl Mannheim as a sociological political theorist.

Some writers have objected that Mannheim's thought represents the negation of political theory rather than, in any serious sense, its

continuation and adaptation.[4] But the defining feature of theoretical political thought is not the moral problem of obligation or the
question of the best constitution or any other such theme. It would
be more appropriate to consider as part of the history of political
theory any sustained attempt to depict a structured relationship
between politics and knowledge; and it would be best to recognize
that various attempts will differ markedly as to the concepts and
problems which appear central, as to the approaches which seem
appropriate, and as to the criteria for correct answers to the questions raised.

Questions about what persons can know and how they can
know it have special weight in political enquiry. They refer, for
example, to that 'recognition' without which authority is inconceiv-
able; they refer to responsibility; and they refer to the 'rationality'
which the most varied political theories locate somewhere in political life and which is supposed somehow to vindicate the coercion
and violence which are everywhere a feature of that life. When
political theorists are quite secure in their answers to questions
about the nature of knowledge, they are likely to construct new
questions which presuppose those answers – as with subtle
enquiries about natural law, and the like. But if the problems of
knowledge themselves require new solutions, then the traditional
topics are likely to be recast so as to reflect these more basic considerations.

The theme of knowledge enters upon our understanding of
political theory at two levels. First, there are the difficulties likely to
arise in showing that political thought constitutes a structure of
knowledge and not merely an assemblage of opinions and assertions.
And second, there are the questions which arise from the tasks
assigned to knowledge within the political world. Mannheim
thought that a sociological approach, grounded on the special boundary position of the social type of the 'intellectuals', could break
through the impasse he found blocking advance in this domain.
What appears to Mannheim as a Copernican new insight into the
nature of political knowledge requires a substantial reformulation of
traditional political concepts and relationships. The sociology of
knowledge offers itself as at once a thorough critique of the prevail-
ing tradition of political thought, charging it with having illusions
about political knowledge and about its knowledge about that knowledge, and as an adequate approach to solving the constitutive problems of that tradition. Beyond the sociology of knowledge, then,
Mannheim offers ways of knowing what must be known in political
life.

Mannheim's earliest work, it must be said, displays little interest in what he then took to be the political domain as such. There he is most concerned to counter the inclusion of all ethical and aesthetic questions within a comprehensive positivist system, which dismisses any responses which cannot be comprehended by the methods of that approach. Envisioning instead a pluralist universe of discrete spheres and spiritual enterprises, he seeks to restore the legitimacy of the older humanist concerns by assigning each its place within distinctive cultural enquiries. In the context of these discussions, the political sphere appears comparatively uninteresting, as an arena for the adjustment of narrow interests devoid of spiritual meaning. But Mannheim soon moves away from this position.

The conception of political thinking which he eventually develops claims a wider field than had conventionally been assigned to it and comes, in fact, to comprehend most thinking other than the strictly technical. At first, though, in the methodological reflections leading up to the sociology of knowledge, he takes practical political knowledge in the narrower sense of humanist statesmanship as paradigm for all qualitative, non-positivist thinking.[5] On the basis of this model of the thought which most interests him, he increasingly stresses the need to understand and develop ideas dealing with matters considered political in the narrow sense while seeking to relocate them in a broader sociological context. He leaves no doubt that he means thereby to incorporate and to correct the treatments accorded political matters by earlier political thinkers. The aim is a knowledge about political thinking and about substantive political matters which builds on the effective political knowledge of practitioners, but which also covers many social and philosophical matters not hitherto recognized as integral to such knowledge.

The sociological interpretation of much philosophy and sociology, paradoxically, reveals the political character of the thought-activities these disciplines document, when, as Mannheim urges, 'political' is taken in a broad sense to refer to all 'activity aiming at the transformation of the world' in accordance with a structured will.[6] When Mannheim traces his own work to the philosophical tradition of Hegel or to the sociological tradition of Max Weber, accordingly, he is not denying its political character, because he usually treats these intellectual achievements as ways of coping with the demands voiced and the issues defined by liberal, conservative, and socialist political ideologies. To view Mannheim in the context of political thought, then, is to take him as he commonly saw himself.[7]

To locate Mannheim in the political field, we begin with a

typically ambiguous note he wrote to himself at some time during the mid-30s: 'Disproportionate development between attitudes and thought: in my understanding I have discerned that liberalism is obsolete, but my attitudes are still at a liberal level'.[8] About a decade before he wrote this note, in his work on conservative thought, Mannheim assigned special importance to a distinction analogous to that between attitudes and thinking. He there distinguishes between the determinate patterns of consciousness through which men mediate their experiences of the world and their conceptualized thinking. He takes the former as embodying formative will; they constitute the animating principles of a 'style'. 'Structural analysis' of a doctrine, he then argues, involves the discovery of the stylistic principle which gives it structure and therewith direction. The 'style' is a plan. In that work, then, he also takes up the possibility of thought which does not rest upon such a structured mode of experiencing, but he treats it as a surface phenomenon, incapable of securing authentic knowledge. Anything like a 'disproportion between thinking and attitudes', from this earlier point of view, would imply an inauthentic condition requiring a shift to bring thought more nearly in line with experiential modes.

As indicated by the language of the note quoted, there was some change in Mannheim's thinking in the years intervening between the two writings. His adoption of the term 'attitudes' is associated with a heightened rationalism, a greater propensity to refer such core beliefs or structuring influences to irrational processes which critical thinking must somehow counter and overcome.[9] But strong ambivalence remains.

Mannheim recognizes the liberal response to the world as a primary reference point for his thought. Like John Dewey, whom he came greatly to admire, he distinguishes between an old liberalism and a new, and dismisses only the former as anachronistic and philosophically inadequate. In his practical political creed, at least, he builds on the tradition of the liberal and reformist movement which was led in the Budapest of his youth by Oscar Jászi. His many departures from that tradition, even when they are adaptations to what he takes to be historical imperatives, can best be understood as part of a search for an inclusive and philosophically grounded way of comprehending liberal calls for reason, reconciliation, responsibility, and personal development. Writing to Jászi in 1936, in response to some criticisms Mannheim says:

I am an old follower of yours and the impressions of my

youth of the purity of your character are so profound that all reproofs I find paternal and they touch me deeply. . . . I find the basic difference between the two of us in one thing. In my opinion, both of us are 'liberal' in our roots. You, however, wish to stand up against the age with a noble defiance, while I, as a sociologist, would like to learn by close observation the secret (even if it is infernal) of these new times, because I believe that this is the only way that we can remain masters over the social structure, instead of it mastering us. To carry liberal values forward with the help of the techniques of modern mass society is probably a paradoxical undertaking; but it is the only feasible way, if one does not want to react with defiance alone. But I am also familiar with such a way of reacting, and it is probably only a matter of time until I join you in it.[10]

When Mannheim arrived at the University of Budapest in 1912, he followed a well-established organizational path which took him from the Galileo Circle, then a club for reform-minded students, to its sponsoring group, a lodge of Freemasons named for a liberal revolutionary, and to the activities of the Social Scientific Society. The reformers avowed themselves 'socialists' rather than 'individualists' on questions of economic organization, but they stressed that their consequent advocacy of state planning and regulation had nothing in common with notions of class struggle or class revolution, not to speak of the dictatorship of the proletariat or the end of the state. The state, they thought, must be strong, liberal, parliamentary, and democratic. Oscar Jászi had written in 1908:

To raise humanity to the highest conceivable level of morality, science, aesthetics, and hygiene – that is the objective. The way to it is through the ever more complete mastery by the human spirit over things. The main idea of socialism, planful cooperation all along the line, is doubtless a more scientific idea than the main idea of individualism. . . . But at the same time there must not be missing that quantum of freedom which determines goals, makes discoveries possible, changes antiquated conditions, precludes arbitrary rule, and makes possible the advancement of the best.[11]

In support of these objectives, the reform group lent its support to the Socialist Party in campaigns for democratic suffrage and political liberalization. Democratization was reconciled with the requirements for 'scientific' policy by confidence in the influence of a dedicated and enlightened intelligentsia. Their authority was to be exercised, above all, through popular enlightenment. At the opening of a 'Free School for Social Studies', soon to be expanded into a program of Workers' Schools supported by the socialist trade unions, Jászi emphasized the non-partisan but also political character of this activity:

> We must . . . make every effort to work out a new morality, a new ethics in place of the decaying old religious or metaphysical one. A new morality, founded on science and human solidarity. . . . One more word about the road to this end. We are convinced that this road can only be the road of free inquiry. The road knows neither dogmas nor party-truths. No socialist party-truths either, it goes without saying.[12]

And indeed, radical intellectuals repeatedly praised these schools for helping to moderate the unreasoning socialist enthusiasms of the masses. While the Socialist leadership saw in the Workers' Schools an instrument for organizing and mobilizing the hitherto unpolitical industrial workers, the lecturers themselves hoped for a different kind of popular education, and they stressed the complex and technical character of problems encountered in managing social change, implying that solutions of these problems require leadership by the well-educated. Shortly before the First World War, Jászi founded the Radical Party. Speaking to a membership meeting, he said:

> Guidance for the ideal politician can only come from the Platonic ideal: an age must come when public life is controlled by philosophers, when men of complete theoretical knowledge and complete moral purity take the lead.[13]

For a few months after the Austro-Hungarian military collapse in 1918, Jászi and many of his closest associates participated in the National Council which attempted to govern Hungary. Characterizing the first proclamation of that body, Jászi subsequently claimed

> that every line is impegnated with a sincerely democratic and socially progressive spirit, and that in the reforms demanded we went to the utmost limits attainable at the then-existing state of the country's economic and cultural

development . . . rule in the state by laboring peasants and worker-masses, under the leadership of the genuine, truly creative intellectuals.[14]

Mannheim soon rejected the philosophical and cultural premises which underlie these formulations. But variations on the substantive themes recur throughout his work; and, in the late thirties, he practically reasserts the whole creed as his own. This provides one fundamental reason for placing his work in the liberal tradition.

PHILOSOPHICAL PROBLEMS OF LIBERALISM

The characterization of the liberal tradition offered in thus sketching the practical political creed which was Mannheim's point of departure and of reference will not satisfy those who define liberalism in terms of 'negative freedom' or 'distrust of political power' or 'individual consent'. But an adequate conception of liberalism as a tradition precludes abstracting some ideas from Locke's *Second Treatise*, Smith's *Wealth of Nations*, or Mill's *Liberty* and treating these as touchstones. The story of liberalism is a story of adjustments in these elements, as they are put in new contexts designed to meet changing conceptions of theoretical knowledge as well as developments in other studies taken as relevant. This is quite apart from the effects of changing political circumstances, which are not of immediate concern.

For the liberal reformers of Mannheim's youth, the most important studies were sociological, and in that discipline the followers of Spencer could not maintain their influence against the impact of French and German investigations. Mannheim complicated the situation by emphasizing the importance of other historical and cultural studies. But he did this not least because he became convinced that the liberalism of Jászi sacrificed vital interests of personal fulfilment because of its deference to a social science he considered positivist and hostile to spirituality. That is, after all, a liberal objection to the prevalent form of liberalism.

Mannheim's reservations have to do with the philosophical framework for liberalism rather than with the practical political creed. The central question turns on the character of scientific political knowledge. An important study by Robert Denoon Cumming on John Stuart Mill and the constitution of liberalism as a tradition has called attention to the profound difficulties which confront modern attempts to think philosophically about liberalism. Cumming suggests that liberalism since Mill has been preoccupied with method, that it has been taken up with a process of adjusting a creed to a set of considerations about ways of holding, discussing, and legitimating political opinions. Taking Mill as the representative liberal, Cumming identifies two central features of liberal ventures in political philosophy: first, the liberal political thinker defines his own intellectual situation as a period of 'transition' or 'crisis' requiring a major reinterpretation of the 'tradition' made up of certain ethical ideals and political ideas; second, the modern liberal believes that in political thought as in politics conflicts are not 'insurmountable', that they represent 'differences of opinion . . . resolvable by some kind of transition and adjustment'.[15]

In the work of John Stuart Mill, these two assumptions run through an assemblage of essays, treatises, and journalistic reports which confront the interrelated methodological issues which Mill himself identifies as central to his concerns:

> In politics, though I had no longer accepted the doctrine of [James Mills's] *Essay on Government* . . . as a scientific theory, though I ceased to consider representative democracy as an absolute principle, and regarded it as a question of time, place, and circumstances; though I now looked upon the choice of political institutions as a moral and educational question more than one of material interests . . .; nevertheless, this change in the premises of my political philosophy did not alter my practical political creed as to the requirements of my own time and country. I was as much as ever a radical and democrat for Europe, and especially for England.[16]

The three central issues recognized by Mill, then, are:

(1) the relationship between political ideas and the requirements of scientific theory: can political ideas be recast so as to reveal them as the outcome of scientific enquiry, or, if not, how can they be thought of as matters for rational discourse and choice?
(2) the matter of appropriateness to time, place, and circumstances: is a theory of history the proper context for moral and political decision, and if so, would this not imply a relativism destructive of the humanist interest in what is proper to human nature?
(3) the question of the extent to which political teachings, as pedagogical components of a pedagogical political order, are

themselves matters of 'moral cultivation' and education: are political discussions themselves to be governed by their pedagogical effects on the discussants and auditors, as in rhetorical conceptions of political knowledge, and, if so, what is to prevent political ideas from becoming either wholly unrealistic or starkly manipulative?

Mill did not solve these problems, and Cumming concludes that liberalism appears condemned to 'a certain eagerness for elaborating . . . methodological precepts and remedial programs for the construction of the science of politics – without actually constructing it'.[17]

The liberal thinkers represented by Jászi believed that they could meet the difficulties raised by Mill:

(1) They thought that science, in the broad sense in which they understood it, generates and vindicates their doctrine. As suggested by Jászi's distinction between 'scientific principles' and 'ethical purity', the needed knowledge may be distributed between distinct sciences of means and ends. Methods of knowing may differ with regard to differing classes of objects, but in principle the whole forms a unified structure comprising universally valid relationships between the subjects and objects of knowledge and it provides the means for answering objectively and without prejudice the questions humankind must address. Formulations of both kinds of knowledge, moreover, are equally theoretical, logical, and demonstrable to unbiased intelligence. For these continental liberals, in short, idealist philosophy provides a conception of knowledge which appears to overcome the difficulties created for Mill by his empiricism, while still comprehending the empirically founded social sciences.

When scientific intelligence addresses itself to the social and political realm, according to this theory, it discovers itself as underlying principle. Things make sense by virtue of the fact that they have been ordered by knowledge. There are two qualifications. The knowledge constituting the empirical social world may be radically imperfect and incomplete; the progress of reason requires whole epochs. And things may sometimes proceed in ways that make no sense, simply on the strength of force and ignorance. Civilization is a progressive task, not a metaphysical given. All this appears as philosophically informed supposition in Kant's *Idea for a Universal History*, but now seems to these thinkers a matter of scientific knowledge, arising from the sociological enquiry initiated by Comte and Spencer. As knowledge becomes more complete, the directing of affairs by those who know becomes ever more feasible, but also more necessary.

Knowledge can have effect in the world, they believe, because those who possess it can with the help of scientific method and philosophy become certain of their own knowledge. Those who will benefit from it, moreover, can accept its authority because popular education will persuade them of its legitimacy and because they will directly experience the benefits of an alliance against those they know to be their oppressors. Democratization, accordingly, destroys the power of obscurantist privilege and opens the way to rational solutions. The dark fears of the tyranny of the majority which distracted J. S. Mill are now seen as due to a failure to appreciate the cumulative character of social rationalization, the ways in which achieved social changes condition needs and beliefs. Industrial workers disciplined by their role in complex industrial processes and organized in strategy-minded unions, for instance, need not be feared as a mob threatening to civilization. Jászi always thought that the experience with the Marxist social movements prior to the Russian Revolution had confirmed the masses' will and ability to subordinate themselves to men of knowledge, notwithstanding what he took to be some mystical elements in the doctrine and some atavisms in conduct. Knowledge can be power because power depends on opinion and opinion can be cultivated. Like their counterparts in Germany, England, France, and the United States, the Hungarian reformers thought they were witnessing the emergence of a popular scientific culture.

(2) In great measure, then, the liberals of the generation before Mannheim referred the difficulties which distressed their predecessors to the special limitations afflicting theory and practice in earlier times. But this does not mean that they made the validity of theoretical knowledge relative to time and place, a function of variable parallelograms of forces. While development and progress are vital elements in the social sciences and while the attainment of knowledge itself progresses over time, in their view, normative criteria are timeless and universal in principle. In the last analysis, Jászi maintained, the formal norms of validity rest on what must be presupposed for a rational and free humanity. Political knowledge will consequently identify different problems and possibilities at different times and places, but the ends in relation to which they are construed as problems or possibilities are themselves universal, and the standards which qualify those identifications as knowledge are valid without reference to historical change.

(3) Similarly, the alleged antinomies between the pedagogical and cognitive functions of theory, between the contributions of knowledge to spiritual and to instrumental progress, morality and happiness, are ascribed to a confused or defeatist frame of mind. Participation in knowledge, Jászi thought, gives self-command and command over events. Knowledge can be inculcated in degrees and by stages, and the simplifications required by popularization in no way need jeopardize the standards constituting genuine theoretical knowledge.

A high level of material civilization, if wrought by free social actors, according to this doctrine, affords resources for cultural creativity and leisure for cultural appreciation. There is no clash between organization for modern innovative productivity and moral improvement. The choices between contrasting emphases which had appeared as dilemmas during the harsh early years of the new civilization, now appear compatible, matters of preferences and timing. Persistent agonizing over the choices is now charged to obscurantist propagandists whose hostility to progress in fact stems from a care for privilege or, at best, from a certain sensibility appropriate enough to poetic genius but lacking all claims on reason.

There are important strategic questions concerning the relationships between moral education and intellectual interests for these thinkers, but they can be answered by political knowledge if asked in rational and specific ways. The questions are not viewed as threats to the structure of knowledge itself. In this respect, as in others, the combination of idealist philosophy and positivist sociology appeared to Jászi and his followers to have enabled their liberalism to overcome the philosophical impasse which blocked Mill.

This summary of the ways in which these Central-European liberals handled the issues which Cumming showed us in Mill is not meant as a caricature. But anyone familiar with Thomas Mann's *Magic Mountain* will doubtless hear the accents of the progressive Freemason, Settembrini, in all this and may well turn away with impatient disdain. That reaction is mistaken. It is in any case not helpful for understanding Mannheim. He is, of course, deeply moved by the sorts of considerations the dark Jesuitical Bolshevik, Nephta, puts before the ingenuous Hans Castorp in the novel.[18] But he does not imagine that these negations are solutions; nor is he prepared to rest in the Olympian distance.

The topics of Mannheim's studies clearly indicate his lifelong preoccupation with the constitutive problems of liberal political thinking, and this provides a second, more profound, reason for emphasizing his relationships to liberalism. Mannheim cannot accept the theory of knowledge advanced by the liberals and consequently reopens the questions they had resolved with its help. (1) Beginning with his doctoral dissertation on epistemology, he recurrently sought to relate the theoretical materials with which he was involved to the philosophical delineation of knowledge and especially to the requirements of scientific theory. (2) The themes of history and historicism are even more pervasive, as are (3) his efforts to specify the ways in which the cultural and pedagogical character of theoretical beliefs and utterances affects their characteristics as theory.

Mannheim always described his own work as a work of transition necessitated by a crisis in the liberal tradition and order, and he made it his avowed objective to develop a synthesis which would acknowledge and comprehend the partial legitimacy of each of the bitterly contending and mutually incomprehending parties making up the theoretical and political fields. His writings throughout display in classical form the characteristic preoccupations which Cumming leads us to expect in liberal thinking.

THE LIBERAL FOUNDATIONS OF 'SYNTHESIS'

In the work of his maturity, Mannheim was greatly influenced by certain aspects of Marxian socialist theory, and he recognized a number of other contestants in the ideological field as well, but his deeper analyses constantly come back to a fundamental opposition between 'liberal' (or progressive) and 'conservative' political thinking and to the need for synthesis between them. In his major historical study of conservative thought, Mannheim offers a revealing contrast between the formative principles of liberal and conservative thinking. Although that work is artfully designed to communicate with conservative readers, the further development of Mannheim's theorizing builds more on the liberal side of the comparison.

Mannheim claims that liberalism is conditioned by a consciousness of the possible, not the actual; that it experiences time as the beginning of the future, not as the end of the past or as eternal now. Things to be understood are put in the context of a projected future or in essential relationship to some universal ideal norm, not in the context of their past or of some immanent tendency. Liberals, according to Mannheim, think of their fellows as contemporaries, as associates in a temporal continuum, not as compatriots sharing some communal space with past and future. Structuralism, Mannheim observes, is a liberal way of organizing knowledge: the liberal seeks to understand things as rationalized and manipulable. The conservative, in contrast, pursues interpretive apprehension and appreciation. Liberals, moreover, experience the world in an abstract way, expressible in theoretical terms, while conservatives respond to concrete, unanalysed complexities. Tied to this, in Mannheim's view, is the liberal's vision of complex entities as assembled from additive individual units and his perception of time as a cumulation of discrete moments.

Mannheim stresses the one-sidedness of the theories based upon liberal experiences and he insists upon the corrective value of conservatism; but the liberal elements are clearly more fundamental to his overall design. Defining situations in terms of the 'next step', structural analysis, theoretical comprehension, the perception of generations and contemporaneity are the major presuppositions of his subsequent work. From that perspective, the critiques of rationalism, ahistorism, and individualism indicate areas requiring adjustment. The liberal elements are the basic ones.

This becomes even clearer in the essay on politics as a science. In it, Mannheim portrays the demand for a science of politics as a major product of bourgeois liberal–democratic thought, while associating himself with that demand quite unequivocally in the essay as a whole. Mannheim observes that liberalism created the 'systemic location' for a science of politics, just as it formed institutions which it imagined would rationalize political conflict, such as parliaments, electoral systems, and the League of Nations. As expounded in the liberal political tradition itself, Mannheim contends, all of these conceptions are afflicted by a misleading 'intellectualism' which grossly overvalues the cognitive power and practical efficacy of abstract thinking oriented to universal laws. What is needed, Mannheim argues, is a more adequate conception of what it means to master the political world by reason and to govern political practice by reason. But he clearly does not advocate an abandonment of the underlying design.

In the original German text of 1929, the continuity between Mannheim's thesis and the basic liberal project is made graphic by Mannheim's use of the term *Plattform*. In criticizing the liberal theory of knowledge, Mannheim remarks, 'it was thus the foremost preoccupation of this style of thought to create a purified platform consisting of knowledge which is universally valid, comprehensible, and communicable'. Such knowledge, Mannheim contends, cannot be. But there can be a science of politics after all and a 'platform' where it will operate. Moreover, he claims, this locus of political knowledge involves persons whose wills are free from constraints, who have political choice or decision before them.[19]

The spatial metaphor is important here. Mannheim is talking about a place to stand, a place where knowledge and choice matter and which in some way commands political life. Older liberal conceptions of scientific politics and parliament are aspects of an inadequate design for such a platform. Mannheim's proposal for political education offers a different design:

> But isn't it desirable and possible to have a form of political awakening which speaks to the comparatively free will which is already and should increasingly become the element upon which modern intellectuals rest? Aren't we simply giving up on a weighty achievement of European history if we fail to make the effort, just at the critical moment, as the party machine threatens, to strengthen the tendencies striving to found political decision on comprehensive orientation? Is political awakening only possible in the form of conditioning? Isn't a will which incorporates criticism also a will, and even a higher form of will, which we may not so readily renounce? ... Or is only preparation for insurrection to be deemed political action? Isn't the continuous transformation of men and conditions also action? ... And can it be that only the will which seeks dynamic equilibrium, which has comprehensive vision, lacks a tradition and form of cultivation appropriate to it? Isn't it really in the general interest to create new centres of political will, quickened by critical conscience? There must be a platform where that which is necessary for such a critical orientation ... can be taught, in a way which presupposes people still searching for solutions, people who have not as yet committed themselves.[20]

But if the difficulties which Mill had identified have not been solved by the proposals of Jászi and his generation, how can the comprehensive vision for such a science come about and gain validity as well as political effect? Mannheim originally intended the essay on politics as a science as starting point for *Ideology and Utopia*, his best-known work, and it is the treatment of ideology elaborated in that study which is supposed to provide the 'organon' for such a science.

Mannheim persistently pursued the hunch that sociology of knowledge is somehow central to any strategy for creating a *rapprochement* between politics and reason, and this pursuit connects his diverse essays in that discipline. Throughout, he believed that such sociology has an important transformative effect on its practitioners: sociology of knowledge calls intellectuals to their vocation of striving for synthesis. It changes their relationship to the parties contending in society, giving them distance and overview.[21] But Mannheim's conception of the specific ways in which such sociology might affect the state of political knowledge fluctuated and changed. There are three main versions:

(1) Sociology of knowledge as a pedagogical but also political mode of encountering and acting upon the other forces making up the political world, serving as mediating force reorienting all vital participants in the political process and generating the synthesis which makes possible the 'next step' in a sequence of human activities having intrinsic value;

(2) sociology of knowledge as an instrument of enlightenment, related to the dual process of rationalization and individuation identified by Max Weber, and comparable to psychoanalysis, acting to free men and women for rational and responsible choices by liberating them from subservience to hidden forces they cannot control because they do not recognize them, and by enabling them to gauge realistically the consequences of their actions; and

(3) sociology of knowledge as a weapon against prevalent myths and as a method for eliminating bias from social science, so that it can master the fundamental public problems of time and guide appropriate political conduct.

Before 1932, Mannheim's work fluctuates between the first two versions: afterwards, and especially after 1933, the third plays a substantially greater role. All three versions can best be understood in the context of the quest for an adequate philosophical mode for liberalism. The shifts in emphasis among them in the course of his English career depend on his accommodation to patterns of thinking in his new English-speaking audiences, on changes of Mannheim's diagnosis of the main obstacles to effective political knowledge, as well as on his changed assessment of the prospects for knowledge, planning and rational rule. With his later conception of 'thought at the level of planning', he comes close to claiming success in the search for a science able to 'contribute', as he writes to Louis Wirth upon the outbreak of the war in 1939, 'both to the interpretation of the appalling events and to the right action'.[22]

NOTES

[1]   A programmatic statement can be found in Mannheim's 'announcement' (1929) written on the occasion of taking over the editorship of the series *Schriften zur Philosophie und Soziologie*, originally founded by Max Scheler and published by Friedrich Cohen, Bonn. There Mannheim writes: 'Collaboration between the two disciplines [philosophy and sociology] should not obliterate boundaries, yet mutual stimulation should be one aspiration. Neither displacing the initially philosophical context of inquiry with sociology nor burying empirical methods under empty speculation in the social sciences can be desirable. Co-operation can have but one purpose, namely that philosophical questions can become a part of this newest level of world orientation in science and life, and that sociology in the attempt to permeate reality empirically keeps its investigative impulses always uniformly centered. Philosopy gives up on itself if it does not deal with contemporary problems, sociology if it loses the center of its inquiry.'

[2]   See, for example, Mannheim's introduction to *Man and Society in an Age of Reconstruction* (London: Routledge & Kegan Paul, 1940).

[3]   Cf. 'A Sociological Theory of Culture and its Knowability (Conjunctive and Communicative Thinking)', in Mannheim's *Structures of Thinking*, ed. David Kettler, Volker Meja and Nico Stehr (London, Boston, and Henley: Routledge & Kegan Paul, 1982), pp. 265–271. See also the excursus on intellectuals in Mannheim's *Konservatismus*, ed. David Kettler, Volker Meja, and Nico Stehr (Frankfurt am Main: Suhrkamp, 1984).

[4]   Among others, Sheldon Wolin, Hannah Arendt, and Robert Nisbet have emphasized the contrasts between the presuppositions underlying sociological concepts and the humanist political tradition. For an influential introductory statement, see Sheldon Wolin, *Politics and Vision* (Boston: Little, Brown &

Co., 1960), chapter 10.

[5] Mannheim, 'A Sociological Theory of Culture and Its Knowability', in *Structures of Thinking*, p. 147.

[6] 'Competition as a Cultural Phenomenon', *Essays on the Sociology of Knowledge* (London: Routledge & Kegan Paul, 1952), pp. 191–229.

[7] On the question of Mannheim's relationship to the tradition, see 'Problems of Sociology in Germany', Kurt H. Wolff, ed., *From Karl Mannheim* (London: Oxford University Press, 1971), pp. 262–70.

[8] Mannheim papers, University of Keele, England.

[9] The note is in German, but Mannheim uses the word 'Attituden', which is not in his earlier vocabulary. In the translation of *Ideologie und Utopie*, 'attitude' appears in place of a number of terms which had earlier comprehended the concept in *Konservatismus*, to which the text refers, viz. 'Haltung', 'Einstellung', and 'Verhaltungsweise'.

[10] Letter of November 8, 1936, Jászi Mss., Columbia University. Translated from the Hungarian.

[11] Oscar Jászi, *Art and Morals*, 2nd edn (Budapest, 1908). Quoted in Zoltán Horváth, *Die Jahrhundertwende in Ungarn* (Budapest: Corvina, 1966), p. 290.

[12] Oscar Jászi, quoted in Harváth, *op. cit.*, p. 135.

[13] *Pester Lloyd*, December 31, 1918.

[14] Oscar Jászi, *Die Lage in Ungarn*, p. 12.

[15] Robert D. Cumming, *Human Nature and History*. (Chicago: University of Chicago Press, 1970), Vol. I, p. 16.

[16] J. S. Mill, *Autobiography* (New York: Columbia University Press, 1924), p. 110.

[17] Cumming, *op. cit.*, pp. 12f.

[18] On the question of the resemblance between Naphta and Mannheim's most admired mentor, Georg Lukács, see Judith Marcus-Tar, *Thomas Mann and Georg Lukács* (Budapest: Corvina, 1982).

[19] Karl Mannheim, 'Ist Politik als Wissenschaft möglich?' *Ideologie und Utopie* 3rd edn (Frankfurt am Main: Schulte-Bulmke, 1952), pp. 108, 147, 141.

[20] *Ibid.*, p. 160. Our translation. There are important differences between the German and the English editions. In the English version (*Ideology and Utopia*, London: Routledge, 1936), for instance, Mannheim speaks of 'interests' not 'wills', and this conceptual shift reflects adjustments in Mannheim's relation-

ship to liberalism. The term 'platform' is also used more sparingly in the English text. Mannheim does not give up his references to liberalism, but he revises his understanding of the tradition.

[21]   See David Kettler, 'Sociology of Knowledge and Moral Philosophy: The Place of Traditional Problems in the Formation of Mannheim's Thought', *Political Science Quarterly*, Vol. 82,3 (September 1967).

[22]   Mannheim to Louis Wirth, September 17, 1939, University of Chicago, Joseph Regenstein Library, Archives, Louis Wirth Papers.

2

The Ways of Knowledge

The starting point for the pursuit of knowledge, according to Mannheim, must be an attempt by the thinker to grasp the intellectual situation of his own time. He must begin his enquiries with the questions and issues which are widely discussed in his own community. Moreover, Mannheim conceded a presumption in favour of the approaches and methods of reasoning gaining strength in the thinker's own generation, and he granted this as much to literary intellectuals and political thinkers as to scientific scholars. Where conflict or incoherence mark the scene, according the Mannheim, the thinker must look for ways of rendering the situation clearer and more productive; he may not deny the integral connections between his own thinking and that of his contemporaries.

Mannheim could not, of course, accept all the knowledge claims of all thinkers whose works he considered; but he characteristically questioned such claims by denying the depth, scope, or duration of their validity, while agreeing that they had indeed managed to grasp a dimension or aspect of things. Much of Mannheim's work classifies various types of knowledge, mapping the routes appropriate to diverse ways of knowing. During his years of expounding and justifying a sociology capable of providing comprehensive orienting knowledge about the situations within which actors can take 'the next step', Mannheim nevertheless always insisted on the value of other kinds of sociological investigations, including those which seek to pattern the social sciences on the model of the physical ones. And during the most productive years of his life, he thought that the sociology he was seeking would come about through interaction with those complexes of political ideas which he designated by the commonly dismissive term 'ideology', but treated in a way that drastically changed the function of that concept.

His earliest philosophical position, influenced by neo-Kantian and phenomenological teachings, is expressly pluralist in character, insisting on the irreducibility of differences in ways of knowing as well as in things to be known. But even when he later came to think that he had found a way of articulating theoretically what he had first described as simply a longing for metaphysical unification, he insisted that the philosophy of history, which was to provide the dialectical synthesis, cannot be deduced or imposed by some all-comprehending super-logic. It must emerge out of the course of ordinary disciplined intellectual life, in all its diversity.

As a practical matter, then, Mannheim remained catholic in his determination to find the kernel of truth in all systems of belief and, above all, in his respect for the findings of disciplined inquiry of all sorts. If there is to be a comprehensive knowledge, it will have to embrace all these enquiries, provide a foundation for their distinctive achievements, and vindicate its own claims by standards as demanding as theirs. There was no shortage in Mannheim's generation of young thinkers seeking for truths more humane and inspiring than those provided by academic scholarship; and the calls for renewal of culture or community and for a politics of wisdom and greatness were clichés of cultural journalism. What distinguishes Mannheim is his intellectual conscience. He was moved by Romantic protests against rationalism and positivism, yet determined to retain what humanity had accomplished at great cost in intellectual effort and ingenuity, even while he explored counterbalancing possibilities. The promise of a comprehensive political vision that would overcome the crisis of disorientation he diagnosed in his time fascinated him, but he searched for a mediating way that could conciliate and marshall all human spiritual energies.

Mannheim never published anything but essays. His best-known works, *Ideology and Utopia* and *Man and Society in an Age of Reconstruction* were collections of essays, different in English and German, and were each expressly announced as assembling 'thought experiments' exploring related but not necessarily consistent theoretical possibilities. Five of his more ambitious treatises were left unfinished and unpublished, except for portions worked into essays. The five works are: 'The Distinctive Character of Cultural–Sociological Knowledge' and 'A Sociological Theory of Culture and its Knowability (Conjunctive and Communicative Thinking)' both now published in *Structures of Thinking; Conservatism*; the manuscripts, no longer available, underlying the posthumous publication of 'Approach to the Sociological Theory of Mind'; and *Freedom, Power and Democratic Planning*. This preference for the essay mode is not the product of diffidence. His theoretical assertions were aggressive enough. But, it seems, he considered the more systematic works premature. He writes in *Man and Society in an Age of Reconstruction*:

> I feel that we should not aim at absolute consistency at too early a stage, when our main task is rather to break the old habits of thought and to find the new keys to the understanding of the changing world. . . . The politician, if he is to gain a following, is forced to draw up a clear and definite programme. But if there is to be a science of politics and of society, there must be no obligation to find a definite solution before the time is ripe. The sociologist must be able to say: 'Thus far have I come and no further: the rest I leave to my successors'.[1]

Mannheim saw himself interacting with a field of intellectual forces and objectifications, for which no English word will serve as well as the German word *Geist*, and he hoped that he could strategically intervene in that field to harness and redirect creative energies active there, recontextualizing and thus reinterpreting achievements already recorded, as well as inspiring new ones. Despite his talk of synthesis and later of planning, all this was for Mannheim a process inherently unfinished, a formative process which no one could control.

MANNHEIM'S WAY TO SOCIOLOGY

Karl Mannheim's first German publication was a 1921 review of Georg Lukács's *Theory of the Novel*, a work he had already read in part in manuscript, as a devoted young follower of the author. In that work Lukács maintained that Goethe wrote his great *Bildungsroman*, *Wilhelm Meister*, in an attempt to mediate between Idealist and Romantic views of the world. Both are shown to have valid insights into the human condition, Lukács argued, but each also presents an unanswerable refutation of the other. The Idealist stresses the great gap between the ideal knowable by reason and the reality encountered in experience, and he calls for a life of heroic self-denying service to the ideal. The Romantic rejects this as devitalizing indifference to the sensations and energies of life and contends that an effort to act in the world as if it could or should meet the demands of abstract reason leads to violence against the human soul and to failure. The Romantic instead concentrates on the refinement of sensibility, seeking an opening to spirituality and to experience, so as to move the soul towards perfect self-realization and contentment. The Idealist in turn insists that such a course bring total subjectivism and loss of all critical standards, bitter disillusionment, or submission to brute facts, glossed over by bogus spirituality. Lukács finds that Goethe sought a way out of the impasse by having his protagonist undertake a self-educational movement through social engagements of different kinds, but he concludes that the effort collapsed because it proved impossible consistently to acknowledge that the social paths followed are only uncertainly and provisionally meaningful, and at the same time fulfil the commitments made. Writing in 1914, Lukács views this failure as a symptom of cultural crisis and looks ahead to a new, authentically grounded culture signalled by the revolutionary writings of Dostoyevsky.

Such a dramatic statement of the principal issues confronting ethical life and intellectual reflection had deep meaning for the young Mannheim. He began writing to Lukács before he was twenty, and one of his letters of that time expresses his heartfelt determination to immerse himself in the life of Dostoyevsky, 'since I feel that a knowledge of his life promises solutions'.[2] The problems for which he seeks solutions are much like those that Lukács was to formulate so elegantly, except that for Mannheim the questions about experiencing and guiding one's life are usually subordinated to questions about the possibility and reliability of the needed knowledge. In the early letter just quoted, Mannheim is still struggling with the choice between criticism and philosophy as the best road to knowledge, and he opts for criticism. But by the time of his review of Lukács's work, he had long given up the hope for some unmediated, Dostoyevskian access to the soul, earlier proclaimed a precondition for criticism, and he had greatly refined the philosophical definition of his central concerns.

The review of Lukács itself effectively sums up what Mannheim had concluded at the outset of his independent intellectual career about the manner in which the great clash between Idealism and Romanticism manifests itself in the contemporary world, especially in the domain of knowledge, and about the ways out of the impasse.

He praises Lukács, first, for recognizing that each of the many ways in which a given object can be known is autonomous and has its own logical structure. An aesthetic view of an object's form, for example, requires that the elements of form be recognized as spiritual entities, interconnected in ways appropriate to such entities, and not, for example, by causal linkages of the sort which might be quite properly invoked if the object were to be explained as a physical field of force. Such pluralism respects the Idealist concern for logical order and structural analysis, but it avoids the reductionism inherent in the modern search for universal abstract laws, in the course of which Idealism in its neo-Kantian form has assimilated knowledge to the model of science, according to the view which Mannheim and Lukács then shared.

Second, however, Mannheim celebrates Lukács's attempt to find a level of interpretation which can account for the emergence of the plurality of enquiries and can reveal the reasons for the variety of logics. Mannheim speaks of this level as a metaphysical one, but agrees with Lukács that it will take the form of a philosophy of history. This form accords with modern expressions of Romanticism, with their acute sensibility for historical experience, but it avoids the subjectivism and relativism with which this has come to be linked. Mannheim thus lays out the two central issues of reductionism and relativism which occupy his philosophical speculations and which he carries forward into his subsequent sociological work. The autonomy of the various domains of knowledge counters the reductionist tendency to bring everything down to a fundamental unified science of the analytically simplest parts, like psychology or materialist sociology. The 'metaphysics' projected is seen to differentiate itself into these autonomous activities, and its theory interprets them 'from the top down'. The possibility of such an integrative philosophy, in turn, counters relativism, while acknowledging diversity and change. Mannheim signals the hope that a way can be found to perform what Hegelian dialectics promised.

And, of course, he manifests a kind of solidarity with Lukács, who was in perilous exile as former Commissar of Education in the Communist Kun Regime. But it was a solidarity of a distinctly non-political kind, disregarding what he knew to be Lukács's departures from the position established in *The Theory of the Novel*.[3]

During the Budapest years, until 1918, Mannheim learned about the central themes and enthusiasms of German neo-Romanticism, including Kierkegaard and Eckhardt, as well as Dostoyevsky, in Lukács's circle.[4] Above all, he took up the idea of a great crisis in culture, with its concomitant promise of a revolutionary renewal. Then in 1918 Lukács proclaimed himself a Marxist, and he published in Hungarian a number of the remarkable Hegelian renderings of Marxist thought, which were subsequently to make such an impression upon non-Marxists, when published in 1923 as *History and Class Consciousness*. Mannheim was fascinated by that work, but never accepted its revolutionary teachings. Nor was he satisfied, as his thinking matured, that Lukács's earlier Hegelianism, oriented primarily to Hegel's aesthetic writings, comprehended enough of modern knowledge to serve as more than an inspiration. As late as 1921, according to the diary of Lukács's most intimate friend, Béla Balász, Mannheim asked to be readmitted to the 'Sunday Circle', which had been reconstituted in Vienna. He was apparently refused, because the now politicized group took him to be someone who only felt safe enough to return to their company now that it appeared that the 'world revolution' was being deferred to an ever more remote future.[5] Mannheim admired and respected Lukács but never associated himself with Lukács as a politician. Mannheim's model in political thinking was Jászi. Lukács inspired his philosophical searches for alternatives to the neo-Kantian rationalism taught at the university and presupposed by Jászi's formulation of progressive liberalism.

Mannheim attempted to orient himself to the postwar intellectual environment in another publication which appeared in the same year as his Lukács review. He characterized the cultural situation in Heidelberg, where he found himself after the defeat of the Hungarian Soviet interrupted his precocious literary career in Budapest, in a way which he adopted in later writings. He dichotomizes the situation and distinguishes antithetical alternatives, which he nevertheless thinks can eventually be brought into structured coexistence. Writing for an emigré Hungarian periodical, he reports that 'the intellectual life of Heidelberg can be measured by reference to the opposition between its two poles'. One extreme consists of the sociologists, following the model of the recently deceased Max Weber, and the other consists of the disciples of the poet, Stefan George. 'On one side,' he writes, 'is the university, on the other the boundless literary world.'[6] The record of his misgivings about the intellectual status of the Hungarian sociologists' ver-

sion of liberalism and his involvement in the primarily literary interests of the circle around Lukács in the earlier years, might make it
seem likely that he too would gravitate to the pole opposed to sociology in Heidelberg.

But Mannheim's comment on the Stefan George Circle suggests an important difference between the literary anti-positivist
movement within which Mannheim had come of age and what he
encountered in Heidelberg, and it indicates some of his reasons for
turning instead to Max Weber's brother, the cultural sociologist
Alfred Weber. He claims that the George circle, despite its many
merits and accomplishments, ultimately fails to contribute to the
transformation of life and the radical renewal of spirit which he
considered necessary. Their humanism proves too literary and con-
ventional:

> The George community . . . is a well-intentioned experi-
> ment of lonely intellectuals trying to solve the various
> problems of spiritual homelessness. . . . They deceive
> themselves with the feeling of having ground under their
> feet. They have drawn inward, covering themselves with
> the blanket of culture, leaving the world out and becoming
> lost in themselves. Life in Heidelberg, protected by hills all
> around, makes them feel that they exist and that they are
> important and effective: it will only take one thunderstorm
> to make them nothing but the symbols of an age gone
> by.[7]

For Mannheim, as for Lukács, the involvement in culture was
bound up with the conviction that the old cultural contents had
become obsolete and lifeless, and thus with a passionate attention to
history as the locus for radical renewal. The problem was to find the
historically apt way of attending to history. In his 1917 lecture on
'Soul and Culture', presented in a lecture series associated with
Lukács's group, Mannheim insists that aesthetic criticism and the
exploration of formal structures were all that could be done in the
present age, despite the radical 'inadequacy' of such cultural
activities, but that this restrictive phase would somehow soon come
to an end. This offers a curiously developmental preparation for a
Dostoyevskian apocalypse, but what is most significant here is the
historical emphasis.

While Mannheim never followed Lukács in his subsequent
conviction that the Communist revolution signified the promised
redemptory crisis, he did move towards Lukács's belief that the

destiny of culture and thus of the recovery of the deep knowledge needed for fulfilment was somehow linked to the social and political awareness of those who were to carry it forward. Now in Heidelberg he develops a renewed interest in the sociological scholars and issues central to the progressive social scientists, but he addresses them in a distinctive way and attempts to meet Romantic objections which had originally drawn him away from progressive social science.

In his brief account of Max Weber in the Heidelberg letter of 1921, Mannheim admires Weber's 'unlimited' social and economic knowledge and his evident calling for a career as a 'political leader', and he regrets that confinement in the university and the town blocked Weber's energies and led to his being known 'as nothing but a scientist'.[8] In later work, Mannheim proposes to bring together the political and scientific vocations into a scientific politics vitally affected by intellectuals freed from the bonds of locality. But that project is only foreshadowed in the early years in Heidelberg. In the language of that earlier time, the problem is to find a way of overcoming the historical forces dehumanizing spiritual accomplishments, including effectual knowledge. The discipline he considers most competent to comprehend these forces is sociology. Certainly in comparison with the illusory cultural haven inhabited by the Stefan George circle, sociology appeared as a place for historical understanding and practical development.

Sociology was quite evidently a strong and growing intellectual and spiritual force, and for that reason alone required attention. Yet, from Mannheim's point of view and in the light of his own earlier development, there was also much about it that was threatening. It had originally appeared as a force dedicated to modes of social progress hostile to the spiritual renovation he considered necessary, and it had propagated methods and standards of knowledge which scorned the spiritual structures constitutive of the works comprising culture. The question then was whether there could be a sociology in the service of culture, a study of humans as historically socialized and evolving beings which would not strengthen the forces of social ossification. Such a study would make intellectuals 'feel that they exist and that they are important and effective' without the deceptive shelters from the world which secluded the followers of Stefan George and rendered them Romantic in the bad sense. But there is a paradox here for Mannheim. How can a sociology comprehend culture and contribute to its renovation, when it appears as the organon of intellectual methods hostile to culture?

Mannheim's movement towards sociology began with three of

the five more systematic studies he left unpublished, two of them philosophically oriented enquiries into the character and methods of cultural sociology and the third an application of his conceptions to the historical formation of German conservatism. The first, 'The Distinctive Character of Cultural Sociological Knowledge',[9] argues that cultural sociology produces its own distinctive kind of knowledge, and Mannheim is as much concerned with restricting the claims of cultural sociology to its own authentic domains as with defending the autonomy of such knowledge against critics. He emphasizes the differences between this sociology and that which figured in the progressivism of the Budapest 'Social-Scientific Society', but also denies that it could lay the foundation for an alternate philosophy of life. Cultural sociology, he maintains, offers a valid interpretation of cultural creations insofar as they are a function of social interactions, but cannot thereby judge their worth. It is dependent, in fact, upon philosophical and other disciplines to specify its objects of study: cultural sociology cannot itself determine whether a noise is music or a sight is art. And it cannot ascertain whether something which has been thought represents knowledge.

In 'A Sociological Theory of Culture and its Knowability',[10] the second of his reflections on the scope of cultural sociology, in contrast, he speaks much more sweepingly about seeking a sociological theory of culture itself and a sociological theory of how culture comes to be known. He projects a process whereby the activity of cultural sociology will in time be seen to have brought into being a comprehensive philosophy of history. The validity of this philosophy would be secured by the fact that it will have grown unforced out of disciplined enquiries into the historical rise and character of human cultural achievements, and especially the various forms of knowledge. Such a philosophy, he expects, will provide the metaphysical ground upon which all validity will ultimately shown to be founded. The possibility which Mannheim had already projected in the Lukács review reappears, now expressly linked to sociological work.

But this projected philosophy is put forward as a sort of regulative ideal, in Kant's sense, in that it is not supposed that it is already reliably known. It is offered as a reasonable projection from what is known, 'making sense' of things from an aesthetic as well as ethical standpoint. Although its contents cannot be as yet established, this philosophy of history as regulative ideal opens enquiry into the interrelationships among the diverse bodies of knowledge which have been attained without superseding them or displacing the disciplines which have brought them into being.

The third systematic study, *Conservatism*, which was accepted as Mannheim's *Habilitationsschrift* at Heidelberg in 1925 and published in part, first in German and posthumously in English,[11] experiments with 'sociology of knowledge' as the most strategic subdivision of sociology of culture. The full text, only recently discovered, shows exceptionally well how Mannheim tried to balance his inclination towards broad speculations about the overall meaning of things, in the manner of Hegel, with his admiration for specific social scientific analyses, like those of Max Weber. But this emerges only when the study, in its entirety, is subjected to a 'literary' interpretation. On its face, and especially in the published versions, this work, unlike the methodological essays on sociology of culture, appears as a disinterested, empirical study of an ideological pattern within a specific historical context, monographically exemplifying the methods of sociology of knowledge, taken as a new academic specialty. Modest in its theoretical claims, it avoids speculations about philosophy of history or reflexive scrutiny of epistemological premises or implications of its own proceedings. None of his other investigations concentrates so exclusively on materials from the past or attends so discriminatingly to the ideas of particular thinkers. In the introductory remarks on method, moreover, Mannheim treats the great methodological controversies with diplomatic tact. If anything, he leans here towards an empirical and explanatory approach, stressing the need for the new discipline to uncover causal linkages between social and cognitive phenomena and warning against the propensity, elsewhere prevalent in the cultural sciences, to be satisfied with interpretive elucidations of congruences among meanings in different domains.

To all appearances, then, Mannheim has put his more adventurous ideas aside, while presenting his supervisors, Alfred Weber, Emil Lederer, and Carl Brinckmann, with a scholarly study far removed from his mental experiments with neo-Hegelian and neo-Marxist ideas. Whatever may be discovered about the deeper levels of meaning in this work, there is no doubt that this surface level represents a substantial part of Mannheim's objective in the effort. For Mannheim, findings which connected social and intellectual phenomena were fascinating and valuable in themselves, quite apart from the deeply interesting larger issues which this enquiry seemed to him to raise, and he repeatedly returned to the problems of analytical technique which he first raised in this work.

In his analysis here, he proceeds in three stages: the first is based on the social history of ideas, the second on a morphological

explication, and the third involves an historical interweaving of tex-
tual and sociological explanations. First, then, Mannheim tries to
account for the central place which political ideology, as a distinctive kind of cultural formation, comes to assume in the spiritual
ordering of human experience during the eighteenth and nineteenth
centuries. On this basis, he considers how it happened that a world-
view centered on the political ideas of conservatives gained prominence after the French Revolution. In making the clash of political
convictions central to the organization of worldviews, Mannheim
changes the more idealistic theory he had earlier developed, on the
basis of reflections on art history, adding consideration of conflict
and structural changes. The explanation for the new ideological
world and for the place of conservatism within it emphasizes the
effects of the dual process of state formation and comprehensive
rationalization. Conservatism crystalizes out of the psychological
attitude of traditionalism among social actors (and some observers)
who experience these new developments as harmful, but cannot
ignore them or simply respond in private, individual ways.
Ideologies comprise the orienting mode appropriate to the newly
rationalized state-centred societies, displacing traditional and religious ways of assigning meanings to the experienced world. Conservatism appears, in Mannheim's first account of it, as a way of thinking
about man and society, which gives weight to certain spiritual as
well as material interests damaged by rationalization but provides a
practical orientation with a measure of effectiveness in the newly
politicized and rationalized world. It thus clearly belongs to the new
time, like its opponents.

Mannheim's second characterization of conservatism seeks to
explicate an inner structure common to the diverse and changing
manifestations of this ideology. Such a 'morphology', Mannheim
stresses, must not confuse what he himself calls a 'style of thought'
with either a theoretical system or a political programme. The structural analysis to be done requires a distinctive method, adequate to
this distinctive kind of object. This method uncovers a characteristic
formative attitude towards human experience in conservative
thought, as it exists prior to any theoretical elaboration, a rootedness
in concrete experience and in particular locales, as well as a special
sense of continuities in time. At a more theoretical level, then, conservative thought stands against all constructions of human relationships which take them as governed by rationalistic universal
norms, like Enlightenment doctrines of natural law. Although Mannheim briefly contrasts liberal and conservative concepts of property

and freedom, he is much less interested in the conservative political creed than he is in the thematic emphases and methods of thinking which he considers constitutive of the conservative 'style'.

Mannheim's third and most ambitious level of analysis traces a part of the formative history of conservatism, with the aim of distinguishing decisive stages and variations in its development and showing empirically how the social and morphological attributes uncovered in the first two treatments interact to shape an historical style and movement. In an introductory overview, Mannheim projects eight stages for this development, but he only writes about two in any detail. In the more finished of the completed sections, he draws on the writings of Justus Möser (1720–1794) and Adam Müller (1779–1829) to present a form of conservatism in which the political perspective of 'estates' hostile to the modern bureaucratic or liberal state acts upon the Romantic thinking which originated among the preachers' sons who form the new post-Enlightenment intellectuals. The second historical analysis deals with Savigny (1779–1861), foremost exponent of historical jurisprudence, whose work is explained as embodying the fastidiousness with which an officialdom having aristocratic connections reacted against schemes of universal codes or universal rights. The ingenuity with which Mannheim works out this analysis, without reductionism of the ideas or arbitrary sociological imputations, has led many sociologists to consider the work on conservative thought as his outstanding achievement, as a paradigm for empirical research into the social genealogy of political beliefs.

But as the work was written, it also manifests Mannheim's preoccupation with the nature of political *knowledge*, not belief alone, and his continuing hope that modes of scientific enquiry can serve as the way to such knowledge without sacrificing scientific devotion to evidence or disinterestedness. The full text shows that Mannheim designed his study of conservatism to serve, at one and the same time, as empirical study and as *exemplification* of several ways of thinking which he presented in the study as characteristically conservative in structure. The idea behind Mannheim's study is that the enduring distinction between natural and historical sciences, as well as the most influential approaches contesting the second of these domains have their historical progenitors in the conservative movement of nineteenth-century Germany. Read from within a conservative 'style of thought', his findings concerning the genealogy of historicist thinking appear as a legitimation of that thinking, including its appearance, in a dramatic change of function, as the method of modern revolutionary thought.

Here, as in several other writings, Mannheim used the literary device of making his essays exemplify the subject matter they are ostensibly viewing at an analytical distance. His essays on 'The Problem of Sociology of Knowledge' and 'Politics as a Science', for example, as well as the second of the essays collected in *Structure of Thinking*, are written in this way. They deal analytically with 'sociology of knowledge' or a 'situational thinking dialectically mediating between theory and practice' or 'dynamic sociology of culture', and they then proclaim, more or less explicitly, that they have displayed the features of the approach under consideration and in some way made it good.

In the complete text of Mannheim's study on conservatism, the situation is more complex, first because the argument is also said to make sense from within an empirical scientific perspective and second because Mannheim analyses and appropriates more than one form of conservative thinking. From Savigny, he derives a model which validates social knowledge on the basis of authenticity of its social roots; from Müller, he takes a conception of practical knowledge rendered adequate by its capacity for making concrete judgements in situations marked by contradictions which cannot be resolved; and from Hegel he abstracts an ideal of a dialectical method capable of generating genuine syntheses which overcome contradictions. The first two of these standards he hopes to meet in what he says about the genealogy and structure of historicist thinking, so that two kinds of conservative arguments in support of historicism appear alongside of the empirically grounded analysis. The last and more ambitious standard is left standing as an aspiration.

Showing the historical roots of historicism counts as a kind of conservative argument on behalf of its authenticity, especially since those roots lie in the progenitors of conservative thought. Balancing morphological and sociological methods, as well as characterizing the present state of thinking as a tense, unstable balance between conservative and progressive – predominantly socialist – elements, counts as a showing of dynamic mediation in the sense of 'synthesis' which Mannheim identified with Müller. Mannheim's academic exercise, in other words, has a level of meaning in which it speaks beyond the discipline, to offer a justification for Mannheim's larger theoretical interests in philosophy of history, even in its Hegelian–Marxist variant, but in a justificatory idiom inoffensive to the academics who are his primary audience.

In the discussion of Hegel scattered through the text, Mannheim suggests that his dialectical way of thinking culminates the development of conservative thought and prepares the way for its transfiguration, when appropriated by new social forces, into an organon for contemporary dynamic thinking. These suggestions are not, however, worked out; the promised section on Hegel was never written. Correspondingly, the level of argument which a 'literary' search for meanings below the academic surface uncovers does not take Hegelian form; Mannheim does not claim to offer a reconciliation between the methodological currents he combines or between the ideological themes he treats. The 'syntheses' remain at the stage of 'mediated' thinking. Mannheim's fascination with Hegel's dialectic is checked by his uncertainty about Hegel's philosophy, his suspicion that Lukács may well be right in treating Marxist revolutionary thought as Hegel's rightful heir, and by his deep respect for the achievements of Max Weber. In *Conservatism*, as in the rest of his work, his business with Hegel remains unfinished.

Mannheim's well-founded failure to settle accounts with Hegel has as counterpart a failure to finish with Max Weber. Mannheim brings Weber into *Conservatism* in a curious and striking way, and he differentiates himself from him in a way equally revealing. In tracing the background of Savigny's thought, in the early nineteenth century, Mannheim comes upon Gustav Hugo (1764–1844), whom he characterizes as representative of a certain kind of hard, hopeless acceptance of a world of facts in which all principles are relative and all developments ultimately fortuitous. Mannheim explains such bitter toughmindedness as a function of a situation in which two competing social strata are evenly balanced and the observer uses the insights of each to discredit the other: 'Here value-freedom, the absence of Utopia, become, as it were, the test of objectivity and proximity to reality'. Mannheim calls this state of mind *Desillusionsrealismus*, and he finds its exact parallel pervasive in German thinking during the time of Max Weber. In its modern form, this realism acknowledges socialist reductions of liberal illusions, but then turns the method of disillusioning against socialist utopianism as well. Max Weber, according to Mannheim, is the 'most important' representative of this style of thinking, and his conceptions of reality and of scientific method are deeply marked by this fundamental attitude.

Mannheim identifies himself with a new generation, destined to overcome such disillusionment. But the overcoming is still a matter of faith and hope and work yet to be done. He concluded his brief excursus on Max Weber as follows:

In periods like ours, in which reflexivity, and a many-sided relativism are reducing themselves to absurdity, as it were, a fear grows up instinctively about where all this will lead. How can relativism be overcome in history? If we can learn from the example [of Savigny], the answer would have to be: not by way of immanent theory but by way of collective fate – not by a refusal to think relativistically, but by throwing new light on new, emerging contents. Here the fact of the generational growth of culture is of immense significance. Although considerable individual latitude is possible, it is phenomenologically ascertainable that the newly growing faith has quite a different character in the most recent generation than it has in those who, coming from an earlier generation, do not take part in this upsurge.

Such a vitalist principle of distinction between himself and Weber could not be his last word. The problem of generations is the subject of Mannheim's next major investigation; and problems of utopia, disillusionment and the mutual discrediting of social knowledge and ideals occupy the succeeding years. The study of conservative thinking exemplifies a technique of analysis which Mannheim acknowledges to be a part of the problem and it experiments with the theoretical uses of literary methods to suggest possibilities for solution. Other experiments are to follow.

STRUCTURES OF KNOWLEDGE

In keeping with his basic commitment to the existing intellectual field as a starting point, Mannheim sought to establish his place in sociology publicly through essays on the currents he considered primary. His inaugural address as *Privatdozent* at Heidelberg was called 'The Contemporary State of Sociology in Germany', and he proposed to the publishing house Siebeck to prepare a collection with the title, 'Analyses on the State of Contemporary Thought', to contain essays on Ernst Troeltsch, Max Scheler, and Max Weber. The intended volume was never published, doubtless because Mannheim preferred to use the materials assembled for the third of these essays instead for the centrepiece in *Ideologie und Utopie*, a volume in a series edited by Mannheim himself. But the papers on Troeltsch and

Scheler, published independently, laid out his position on the prospects for philosophy of history and sociology of knowledge, taking up the conclusions of his more systematic unpublished studies without exposing the full philosophical underpinnings expounded there.

Instead of such a systematic approach, Mannheim accepts the works of the writers he treats as achievements which define the state of the question and then presents his distinctive proposals as extensions or corrections of these seminal works. While negotiating with the publisher, Paul Siebeck, about the intended volume of essays, Mannheim insisted that he could not, as Siebeck had suggested, rewrite the essays so as to give them greater unity, because, he maintained, they were meant to retain their diversity, as conscientious responses at different moments to different aspects of the field.

The essay arising out of his preparations for the Max Weber chapter in the proposed Siebeck volume, 'The Prospects of Scientific Politics', argues the central thesis, that the way to generate the comprehensive social knowledge able to diagnose the historical situation and thus able to ground scientific politics is to examine the contemporary situation in knowledge about society. It then proposes to operate on the conflicting perspectives such an examination reveals, by means of a sociological interpretation. To understand why Mannheim thought that such study could provide an 'organon for politics as a science', and not simply a chapter in the social history of ideas, it is necessary to review the argument of Mannheim's most technical philosophical work, 'Structural Analysis of Epistemology'.[12]

Mannheim claimed that 'structural analysis' of the 'theory of knowledge' was designed less to offer a distinctive theory of knowledge than to lay down the forms, constituent elements, and concerns characteristic of every such theory. Central to his argument, and reminiscent of the distinction made earlier between liberalism as political creed and liberalism as structure of knowledge, is the contention that the theory of knowledge is not a substitute for methods of knowing appropriate to the various enquiries. The theory of knowledge is a justificatory, legitimating enquiry, explaining how it is that something which has been thought can be considered knowledge. It answers the question, '*How* is knowledge possible?', not, '*which* knowledge is possible?'. It cannot pose as a judge over other enquiries, since its own claims rest on foundations no more secure than theirs. In a striking departure from the Cartesian conception, the theory of knowledge is taken as simply one of many constellations in the spiritual firmament, capable of shedding its own glow upon the others; it is not the lens through which the universe is scanned.

The primary consequence of this conception, and its point, is to deny the claim that only those thoughts can be classified as knowledge which can be placed within a system of propositions having certain universal properties, or which can be subjected to a certain kind of universal validating procedure. His argument is aimed against neo-Kantian criticisms of substantive aesthetic, ethical or historical particularity, and also against positivist strictures attacking all knowledge claims which lack a certain kind of empirical verifiability. But it is also aimed against Romantic denials that any sort of structure or critical discipline pertains to many kinds of statements about the way things are or should be. The structural analysis of theories of knowledge, according to Mannheim, enables us to ascertain what theories of knowledge require in order to qualify a thought as knowledge and, because theories of knowledge are a kind of knowledge too, it gives us an example of the effects achievable by subjecting thoughts to such a legitimating procedure.

In addition to the competing Idealist and Romantic world views, and the philosophical schools and political creeds corresponding to them, Mannheim always also has in mind the way in which the literary intelligentsia, which he calls 'impressionistic', treats ideas. He speaks of it as 'a brilliant, often very profound world of independent scholarship and aestheticism, which often loses itself in untestable vagaries, however, because it lacks inner or outer constraining bonds' and he contrasts it to 'a scholarly world, constrained by its academic positions and mastering its materials but removed from the living center of contemporary life'.[13] By way of his analysis of theories of knowledge Mannheim hopes to show that findings which touch vitally upon life are not the products of undisciplinable intuitions. They can be situated, as distinctive forms of knowledge, within appropriate frameworks of knowledge, which will then show how to treat them, so as to prevent their floating and dissolving as vague impressions.

Once we consider something which is thought as something which is known, we become aware of several new things about it. In the first place, we acknowledge that it has its place within a structured universe of thinking, interlinked with other thoughts about specifiable aspects of things. A judgement about the metre of a poem, for example, now appears as an aesthetic judgement, related to other judgements about this and other forms. Secondly, we are led to enquire about the method of criticism and validation appropriate to it. The method itself depends on the structure in question and is not given by the conception of knowledge. But the propriety of subjecting thoughts, even when they are in spheres not normally considered 'theoretical', to appropriate criticism is thereby established. Thirdly, we render the thought normative when we legitimate it as knowledge, i.e. as entitled to set the standard for thinking about what it is thinking about. It moves from being a more or less correct statement, within the framework of the enquiry to which it belongs and subject to the methods of judgement and correction appropriate to that sphere, and becomes a claim. If we want to know something about the metre of a poem and not just find out what aestheticians or critics think about it, we must consider judgements as knowledge.

Mannheim offers a conception of knowledge designed to alter profoundly our attitudes and responses to statements of all kinds about all sorts of things, opening us to the possibilities for orderly and testable thinking about matters otherwise thought subject merely to inchoate intuition or vague supposition. He is not providing us with new methods for judging those things, but is giving us new reasons for paying attention to the methods already in use or under consideration among those knowledgeable in the relevant domain.

'To know', Mannheim writes in his essay 'On the Interpretation of *Weltanschauung*', 'is to gain a kind of possession of the matter before us which allows us to orient ourselves in relation to it and to master what we have gained.'[14] In German as in English, Mannheim's language suggests a strong connection between knowing and purposing. Although the terms of appropriation and command need not refer to pragmatic uses in any narrow sense, knowing appears as an activity within a design. It is up to the theory of knowledge to explain the elements involved and their precise relationships.

From the standpoint of all such theories, according to Mannheim, the key elements are always, first of all, a subject and an object of knowledge. To explain the relationship between them, Mannheim contends, theory of knowledge requires the assistance of a 'foundational science', notwithstanding the claims of many theorists in this field that they are proceeding without presuppositions. He finds only three disciplines able to serve in this way. Psychology characterizes subject, object, and their interconnections in the language of psychological events; logic construes them as patterns of necessary relationships; and ontology uncovers the structural unity of the ultimate ground upon which all three elements rest. Although Mannheim at times professes to be neutral toward the different possible epistemological theories, which he elaborates with considerable ingenuity, he implicitly endorses ontology, since his structural analysis of theories of knowledge proceeds precisely as, he insists, a theory founded upon ontology would have us treat anything that is claimed to be known.

Mannheim contends that every such claim can on reflection be referred to some 'systematization' in which it is 'at home'. The domains of knowledge in question may well fail to coincide with the disciplinary boundaries which happen to have been established in the course of cultural history. But they can be identified because each possesses a unifying animating spirit, a 'will to discipline', a purposive design, or a meaningful plan. Knowledge exists, on this theory of the relationship, when the knower connects with the aspect of things upon which a given structure of knowledge is grounded. Mannheim speaks of 'premises' in this connection, but makes it clear that he is using the logical term in an extended sense when he goes on to say that these are 'premises which a person, so to speak, has to accept, acknowledge, approve, and is party to whenever he states a theoretical concept in a meaningful way or somehow directs his attention to it'.[15]

We reflect on what we think or on what someone claims to know first of all by becoming aware of the context in which it belongs and then by somehow finding our own place within that same context. Once oriented, we will know also how to characterize and to test what seems known in the manner appropriate to the domain. It is the controllable experience of appropriateness which makes the decisive difference. As the example of Mannheim's structural analysis of theories of knowledge is meant to show, such insight will also identify the limitations of the domain, its inability to supersede the autonomy of others.

Mannheim distinguishes three classes of systematizations with distinctive kinds of structures. Art contains systematizations in which integrity of form counts but alternative possibilities in no way exclude or even criticize one another; science, in contrast, comprises rigorously logical systematizations for which, in principle, there are uniquely correct questions and answers; and philosophy is intermediate between them. Its constitutive enquiries, according to Mannheim, must be understood to have correct solutions in principle, if the point of doing philosophy is not to be denied, but alternative proposals can never be wholly rejected since they somehow contribute to knowledge. The enquiries, in any case, may be so important to human purposes that it is unthinkable to suspend judgement until some time in the future when the ultimately correct solution may appear. Approximations and circumscriptions must be allowed to serve, so long as they can be shown to be properly grounded.

In general, then, Mannheim's ontological theory of knowledge states three tests for the legitimacy of something put forward as knowledge. First, it must somehow perform the mastering and orienting functions of knowledge. Second, it must be authentically grounded in the being about which knowledge is claimed. And third, it must have properties congruent with the structure of the systematization to which it belongs; i.e. the concepts in which it is formulated and the relationships said to exist between them must fit the respective type of reality. In the philosophical treatise in which these vague tests are developed, they gain somewhat greater force because, although persistently formulated in the metaphorical language of 'place' and 'home', they are tied to powerful philosophical tendencies associated with such influential thinkers as Husserl and Heidegger, and because they are offered as challenges to highly respected philosophical doctrines which are intelligently analysed and criticized.

But their main interest in the present context is that they provide a general framework within which Mannheim subsequently addresses the problem of social and political knowledge. His strategy for overcoming the reductionism and relativism endemic among the approaches characteristic of his time, and therefore not to be dismissed out of hand, depends on the possibility of crystallizing structures of thinking out of the sea of opinion, mapping them, and then finding a way to link them in a coherent design. The method of 'structural analysis' exemplified in his work on theories of knowledge is supposed to make this possible.

SOCIOLOGY OF KNOWLEDGE

Two developments mark Mannheim's turn from the more general attempt to establish ontological grounds for the constitution of all kinds of cultural knowledge to the more specific design for uncovering the social bases of ideologies. These are the common elements in the essays intended for the 'Analyses of the Contemporary State of

Thought', which were Mannheim's responses to Ernst Troeltsch's *Der Historismus und seine Probleme* (1922), Georg Lukács's *Geschichte und Klassenbewusstsein* (1923), and Max Scheler's *Versuche zu einer Soziologie des Wissens* (1924). The first development is an inclination to treat social reality as the last knowable reality and thus to consider the ultimate social identity of cultural entities, including knowledge of all sorts, as indicating their place in the order of things.

Since he views that social reality as undergoing continual historical change, this contention represents a departure from his structural analysis of theories of knowledge in one important respect. There he expressly denies the possibility of history in any form serving as a foundational science in the sense of psychology, logic, or ontology. But this departure is clearly in line with his earlier fascination with the possibility of a philosophy of history as a comprehensive frame of reference for all interpretation. And it marks his response to the exciting interplay between Marxist theories of ideology, given unprecedented new subtlety in the writings of Lukács, and the more spiritual sorts of cultural sociology associated with Alfred Weber as well as Scheler.

Mannheim shared with more than one philosophical generation in Germany the idea of somehow reconciling, in a philosophically apt way, the Romantic insight into the flux of things and the Idealist vision of a rational order. The philosophical journal which brought into collaboration a group of thinkers ranging from Heinrich Rickert and Max Weber to Edmund Husserl and Friedrich Meinecke graphically signalled this design on every volume: there was on it an embossed head identified as Heraclitus and the title *Logos*. Lukács published in it, as did Mannheim himself; and the journal *Szellem*, which Lukács had originated and where Mannheim got his start, was to have been an Hungarian pendant to *Logos*, similar to one which saw several editions in Russian. Like the other serious scholars assembled in *Logos*, Mannheim recognized that agreement on a common problem, loosely stated, and a common goal is not the same as a solution or even an agreed way. In the years between 1923 and 1930, however, Mannheim thought that he had struck upon a strategy that could serve. The philosophical statement of this response never achieved a formulation that satisfied Mannheim, but the regulative ideal of a dynamic social ontology governed much of the best-known phase of his work

Congruent with this decision, Mannheim turned away from the concept of *Weltanschauung* which had been central to his earlier explication of cultural sociology as a specialized discipline. He now decided that social–political ideology constitutes the core cultural and spiritual formation of the modern age, at least since the French Revolution, and that other formations can best be interpreted as structurally related to ideology. Accordingly, he expressly recognizes social ontology as itself a way of proceeding which is best understood in relationship to the conservative and socialist ideologies from which it springs. He also acknowledges that the construction of experience as socio-political in structure cannot be shown to be more than an approach historically appropriate to the present day.

He nevertheless insisted that these limitations on our knowledge need not jeopardize its status as genuine knowledge. They do not deprive us of the ability to test and to improve it. The possibility of a comprehensive social knowledge about the interrelationships among the various ideological forms of social knowledge, grounded on an understanding of their interconnections at other levels of social reality, promises a new way of knowing and a new way of society. Politics as a science is now possible.

Mannheim claims that the sociology of knowledge constitutes the 'organon for politics as a science'. This means that it provides a method of operating on the ideological views active in politics so as to give them a new character, constituting a field of knowledge having a structure appropriate to this dimension of reality and to the work that knowing performs within it. In his famous lecture on 'Politics as a Vocation', which Mannheim always had in mind as he worked on these materials, Max Weber had made a profound distinction between the uses of words in politics and in science, likening the former to weapons for overpowering opponents and the latter to plough shares for cultivating knowledge. Mannheim offers the sociology of knowledge as a way of bringing about the biblical transformation of swords into pruning hooks, which had been prophesied by Isaiah.

Although Mannheim invokes Weber's conception of politics as dependent ultimately on choices which no knowledge can dictate, his own conception of the insight to be derived from comprehensive understanding of the political situation and his extension of the clarifying impact which authentic political knowledge can have upon the political field of action fundamentally alter the meaning of the Weberian formulas he invokes. When Weber applies another of Isaiah's sayings, about watchmen in the night, he wants to reproach those who wait in vain for prophets to save them, instead of soberly meeting the demands of the day. Mannheim invokes the same images to call intellectuals to a mission of guardianship.[16]

In his study of conservatism, Mannheim had cited Weber as exemplary representative of an heroic realism of disillusionment (*Desillusionsrealismus*), and distinguished his own generation from that condition, by virtue of their experience of new promise. The great critical discoveries and achievements of the earlier generation, he believed, were to be taken up but now given a new, essentially positive function. Mannheim credits Weber with showing that the Marxist method for unveiling the social provenance and function of political ideas applies equally to their own view of the world. Now this method is to reveal its constructive powers. The ways in which Mannheim supposes this transvalued method to proceed corresponds to the legitimating and indeed transformative tests he ascribes to the theory of knowledge.

The essays published in 1929 in *Ideologie und Utopie* should be taken together with Mannheim's work on conservatism, his presentation on 'Competition as a Cultural Phenomenon' to the Sixth Congress of German Sociologists in Zurich in the autumn of 1928, which initiated the sociology of knowledge dispute,[17] and his handbook article on the sociology of knowledge, published in 1931. In all of these writings, there is the characteristic recognition of plurality in the intellectual field, along with a new emphasis on competition among intellectual designs, and there is the notion of an intellectual strategy for furthering a comprehensive overview which will at least give the competitors an awareness of a common direction of social movement and some shared conception of overall meaning. The overview may even render the contests anachronistic.

Mannheim's strategy involves two steps. First, the great variety of ideas in the modern world is classified according to a scheme of historically given ideological types, few in number, in keeping with Mannheim's thesis that the ideological field has moved from a period of atomistic diversity and competition into a period of concentration. Liberalism, conservatism, and socialism are the principal types, with fascism and bureaucratic conservatism also receiving some mention. Second, each of these ideologies is interpreted as a function of some specific way of being in the social world, as defined by location within the historically changing patterns of class and generational stratification. Liberalism is thus referred to the capitalist bourgeoisie in general, and various stages in its development are referred to generational changes. Similar analyses connect conservatism to social classes harmed by the rise of the bourgeoisie to power, on the one hand, and socialism to the new industrial working class, on the other.

Each of the ideologies is said to manifest a characteristic 'style' of thinking, a distinctive complex of responses to the basic issues which systematic philosophy has identified as constitutive of human consciousness, such as conceptions of time and space, the structure of reality, human agency, and knowledge itself. The political judgements and recommendations which make up the surface of the most purely ideological texts must be taken in that larger structural context. This is not to say that every ideology elaborates such a philosophy, or, indeed, that the elaborated philosophies associated with an ideology can be taken as providing an adequate account of the underlying ideological structures. Such philosophies are ideological texts like others, and require structural analysis and sociological interpretation in order to be truly comprehended. The style of thinking, according to Mannheim, becomes most evident in the ways concepts are characteristically formed and in the logics by which they are interlinked. These are the features which must be analysed in order to discern the distinctive style.

Each of the styles, in turn, is said to express some distinctive design upon the world vitally bound up with the situation of one of the social strata present in the historical setting. Mannheim is emphatic, in his original German texts but not in his later English revisions, that this design cannot be simply equated to a group 'interest', because he disavows the theory of motivation associated with the stress on interest. He does speak of the 'aspirations' of groups or of other social entities in this connection, but he does not hold that testimony by group representatives about demands or wishes is necessarily definitive. The sociologist of knowledge has no direct authoritative information about the formative will, which he postulates as the principle of integration and immanent development in ideological wholes. The self-explanations which groups set forth in their ideologies and utopias are the starting points for knowledge about underlying styles and principles, along with such social theories as may be available concerning the logic of their social location.

The sociologist of knowledge then works back and forth between these two sources to uncover the interpretation he is seeking. So, for example, the very definition of a generational unit, which may serve as a point of reference in the social interpretation of an ideological phase, depends on evidence that a given historical experience has in fact become a central point of reference for the cohort that went through it. Similarly, the definitive importance of a given social or political demand for a given social group – or indeed the saliency of social identity to social knowledge – cannot be established without using information about ideas associated with the group to elucidate other sociological or historical data, as well as without moving in the opposite direction. Mannheim is aware of the circularity here but denies that it is damaging to his undertaking, since he is not striving for causal explanations of social belief or social knowledge but for explications of such knowledge in the context of a comprehensive or 'total' view of the society undergoing change.

It is the view of the 'totality' which is the real point of the study. Sociology of knowledge seeks to give an account of the whole ideological field, in its historical interaction and change, together with an account of the historically changing class- and generational situations which the ideologies interpet to the groups involved. To have a method for seeing all this, according to Mannheim, is to have the ability of seeing in a unified and integrated way what each of the ideologically oriented viewers can only see in part. It is to have the capacity for viewing the situation as a whole.

Mannheim's essay on politics as a science illustrates this procedural conception. In it he treats the ways in which each of the ideologies sees the relationship between theory and practice, inter-relating his findings with characterizations of the social reference points for each ideology. In the course of that exercise in sociology of knowledge, he introduces the concepts which he then uses to characterize politics and the role of knowledge within it. Many readers of Mannheim object that his analyses presuppose a sociological philosophy of history which he does not sufficiently expound or defend, but Mannheim sees the interpretation of the historical situation as the product of his treatment of the ideologies and validated only to the extent that this treatment brings it forth.

In all this, the concept of 'situation' has special importance for Mannheim. To comprehend a piece of the historical world as a 'situation' is to see it in the way that a foresightful and perspicacious political actor sees it. The concept already appears in that form in Hegel's lectures on aesthetics, where the world as 'situation' refers to the world as possessing moral significance, as a scene for action. A situation comprises a complex of factors and conditions; it is charged with meaning: opportunity and prospects, threat or promise.

In a sense, then, the sociologist of knowledge seeks the same kind of knowledge as the ideologist. He acquires the intellectual means for effective political action. The major difference is that he has a larger view than the ideologist, a synoptic vision. He is able to diagnose his time. And, Mannheim insists, he is no mere spectator.

A spectator could not, in any case, read situations. That persupposes a will or design.

But the problem of the precise character and source of the 'will' energizing and directing the 'style' of sociological thinking troubles Mannheim in these writings, and it is one of the important features with regard to which the different essays venture different experiments. Although he acknowledges that the key concepts of the sociology of knowledge derive from Marxist social theory, which he considers to be an explication of proletarian socialist ideology, he maintains that the terms as well as the procedures in which they are employed undergo a basic change in design when they are made part of the sociology of knowledge. No longer employed as a technique for discrediting and demoralizing opponents, the new understanding brings out the cognitive capabilities of ideologies even while uncovering the ideological character of social knowledge. These differences make it impossible to consider the proletariat and its social purposes as the force behind sociology of knowledge.

Nor can sociology of knowledge be seen as animated by the universalist and rationalist designs which Mannheim considers congruent with the social location of the capitalist bourgeoisie and which he identifies as the social principle of liberalism, because sociology of knowledge emphasizes the historically bound nature of social knowledge as well as the residue of volition and choice in all understanding. After excluding, for similar reasons, the other primary social styles and their social authors, Mannheim suggests, since he has no doubt that sociology of knowledge is a rising force that cannot be stopped, that it must express the designs which distinguish the urbane and educated intellectual stratum which is bringing it into being and actively responding to it.

But Mannheim himself raises a number of difficulties with this suggestion. First of all, it is not clear how intellectuals can be the source of a distinctive creative political design of their own, since they are the elaborators of all the ideologies, in the service of all social impulses. He speaks of them in this connection as natural apologists for all groups. Mannheim meets this difficulty by suggesting, to begin with, that even their justifications for others raise social and political impulses to a level above brute conflict. They bring clashes of interest and struggles for power into the sphere of the spirit and thereby reproduce and develop the cultural inheritance. Their conversation with that field, moreover, and their exchanges with one another in the language of the educated, notwithstanding their differing ideological affiliations, gain a special weight in a time when there is a dramatic concentration and polarization of the competing ideological forces, as Mannheim believed there to be in the late 1920s.

Because the intellectuals are situated where the ideologies make their competing claims in the most sophisticated ways, they are well-placed to become aware of the plurality of ideologies and of the intellectual power they severally possess. Mannheim illustrates this point in his own practice by referring with respect to Lukács, Lenin, and even Stalin, on the Left, and to Othmar Spann and Vilfredo Pareto, on the Right. The prime social class competitors themselves, in contrast to the intellectuals, become ever more rigidly organized and steadily more distrustful of 'their' intellectuals. They are satisfied that the time has come for confrontation rather than competition over the public interpretation of the world, and they find that intellectuals, whatever their ideological profession, jeopardize the combativeness of the parties to which they adhere. All this, in Mannheim's view, weakens the links between many intellectuals and the vital principles animating the ideologies around them. They come to an increasing awareness of their distance from the actively engaged organizations and their commonality with other intellectuals.

But that raises the question whether this distancing will not simply lead intellectuals to function, as they have done from time to time in the past, as sceptics and relativists, as pessimists about all action, or as fideists in defiance of their own knowledge. Mannheim thinks that these possibilities can be discerned in the great examples of Dilthey and Simmel, Weber, and Scheler. He argues, however, that the new generation, of which he is part, has witnessed the innovative political achievements of the postwar period and that this generation consequently envisions new possibilities for action. Mannheim avoids concrete political references, but he seems throughout quite hopeful about the Weimar political situation. As late as 1932, he speaks about a politics of conflict and compromise among contesting interests and ideologies in a tone markedly more positive than the political commentary of almost all of his academic colleagues.[18] Such passages must be balanced, of course, against other passages proclaiming a great crisis in political and social life. But in their bearing on the question of the purposiveness of the intellectuals, the two readings of the political situation converge in their effects. Promise and threat together stimulate the intellectuals to action on their own behalf, Mannheim thought.

This should not be misunderstood. Mannheim was not suggesting that intellectuals could or should seek political power for themselves or even attempt to generate a distinctive new course of social development. The special mission of the intellectuals, as Mannheim saw it, was to work for 'synthesis': to cultivate a political life in which the 'next step' in the historically conditioned line of development can be taken with minimal loss to old achievements in culture and maximal enlistment of all social energies. They were to bring about, in other words, what liberal ideology had claimed for the market place of ideas and parliament – except that they were to understand and to show what needs to be done to that end in a world more complex, irrational, and activist than that which liberalism projects.

During the period reviewed here, Mannheim maintained that the sociology of knowledge is central to this task. But even then, he explored at least two possible ways in which this knowledge could work. Although it is the second of these which received primary emphasis in his later work, especially after his emigration to England, it is the first which grew more directly out of his philosophical development and which has been discussed so far. This line of argument makes sociology of knowledge the vehicle for generating and rendering politically effective a comprehensive social knowledge, synthesizing what the ideologies have only partially seen.

And Mannheim contends that there are historical precedents for intellectuals assuming a mediating role. Even if there has never been a prior instance of a mediation incorporating all the ideologies present in a competitive field, according to Mannheim, the great variety of ideological ventures which crowded the field after the breakdown of the old monopolistic control over the public interpretation of social life exercised by the Church were concentrated into the very small number of present-day ideological competitors by the achievements of such synoptic thinkers as Stahl and Hegel, for the conservatives, and Marx, for the socialists. He finds, moreover, that the work of thinkers like Ernst Troeltsch and Alfred Weber, who expressly direct themselves to the public realm as well as to the academy, indicates that such a sense of mission is in the process of formation.

Mannheim spoke of these matters in a language adapted from Marxist conceptions of class consciousness. The point of the discourse was not simply to show that the developments described were in fact under way, but also to make intellectuals recognize that what was being said made sense of their own experiences, lives, and aspirations, and thus to bring them to acknowledge that they share in this mission. Their own subsequent interventions, in turn, proceeding through the findings of sociology of knowledge, would not simply uncover new information about things in the social world. By redefining the situation in ways which directly involves the vital energies of the contesting ideological parties, they would be changing the structure of the political field.

The most distinctive feature of Mannheim's approach in these writings, then, is neither the social interpretation of political ideas nor the extension of that concept to a wide range of cultural productions not usually considered political. This he accepts as the achievement of a whole line of thinkers, culminating in Marx and Weber. Mannheim makes two claims, however, which are distinctive.

First is the conception of ideologies as cognitive structures. They are variously flawed, limited, perspectivistically one-sided, subject to drastic correction from other perspectives, but nevertheless productive of knowledge. Mannheim does not understand the structure of ideologies as an organization of recommendations and claims built around some central 'value', as is commonly done now; he emphasizes their implicit 'ontologies' and 'epistemologies'. Nor does he assume, as others do, that every ideology is to be understood as built upon some conception of human nature; instead, he stresses their conceptions of historical development and of the relationship between knowledge and action.

The second original claim which Mannheim makes is that sociology of knowledge bears on the substantive issues that ideologies address and contributes directly to political orientation. It does so, in his view, not because knowledge of social genesis can in itself determine judgements of validity, but because enquiry into social genesis will, if comprehensively done, bring about a synthesis of valid elements in the ideologies, relocating them in a developmental context which will not so much falsify the ideologies as cognitive structures as render them obsolete – displaced by a new comprehensive vision.

The word 'method' derives from the Greek work for 'way'. Although contemporary usage takes method as referring primarily to the procedures to be followed in enquiry, there is an older sense, preserved in some contexts, in which method may also indicate the topics or 'places' which an enquiry must traverse in order to reach its objective. Mannheim's sociology of knowledge is a method for attaining political knowledge in the second of these senses. By requiring the investigator to explicate the diverse intellectual formations competing in the ideological field, correlating them with one another and with the situation in the society within which the ideological field is located, the study carries the enquirer through the matters he must consider in order to interpret the situation of his time. And it is a method or way in a third sense: the enquirer who pursues this course gains a new readiness for comprehensive knowledge. He is freed from illusions about the various ideologies and he experiences a new form of mastery. While Mannheim's confidence in the former significance of sociology of knowledge is subjected to considerable strain and is eventually overcome by counter-currents, the second one forms the basis for a continuing claim.

TWO CONCEPTIONS OF IDEOLOGY

Mannheim had distinguished three features as distinctive of knowledge in its various types. There is first a quality of authenticity, a rootedness in some lasting relationship to a dimension of reality. Aesthetic knowledge, for example, was seen to rest on a responsiveness to form, and form was said to have real existence, in the special way that meanings exist in the world. In his studies on the sociology of culture as a mode of knowledge, now published as *Structures of Thinking*, Mannheim sought to uncover comparable structured attitudes and ontological objects to account for the possibility of the knowledge he was examining there. Second, then, knowledge is situated within an integrated structure, distinguished by its manner of forming concepts and by its logic. So, for example, the whole class of physical sciences operates with univocal universal concepts interlinked in deductive logical systems, while cultural sciences employ descriptive concepts connected in more uncertain ways. Third, knowledge provides what Mannheim calls 'orientations' to a given domain, and knowledge can be applied, recalled, and transmitted in some way. Transient impressions and idiosyncratic intuitions thus cannot count as knowledge, although systematizations will differ in the degree to which they can make use of such mental acts. Mannheim's conception of sociology of knowledge as organon for a science of politics builds upon all three features of this theory of knowledge. The tests that it generates, however, also help to explain Mannheim's uncertainties about the conception and his continued interest in quite a different reading of the character and importance of a sociology of knowledge.

The two currents in Mannheim's thinking about the sociology of knowledge have caused difficulties for his many commentators, who have been curiously unwilling to take seriously Mannheim's admission of inconsistencies in his work, or even to explore systematically what he might have meant when he insisted on his right to pursue alternative possibilities. His German contemporaries reacted to the more ambitious conception of sociology of knowledge as organon, while later writers, especially English-speaking ones, have concentrated on his notion of the sociology of knowledge as (also) a positive discipline, a specialization within academic sociology.

The problems are compounded by the fact that Mannheim does not strictly reserve the alternative possibilities for separate treatment in distinct essays. While there are differences in emphasis from essay to essay and a shift in emphasis after the 1920s, the conceptions are frequently intertwined. Mannheim sometimes speaks of them as representing, in effect, his maximum and minimum programs. But this formula does not really cover the situation, since the conception of sociology of knowledge as discipline differs from the conception of sociology of knowledge as organon precisely with regard to the two points which have been noted as Mannheim's distinctive claims: the cognitive character of ideologies and the bearing of sociology of knowledge on the generation of substantive theory of history. The countercurrent in Mannheim's thinking functions rather as a fall-back position, designed to preserve what appear to be valid findings and practices of sociology of knowledge, while avoiding theoretical and political difficulties associated with his more ambitious design.

To speak of 'programme', 'position', and 'political difficulties' in this connection is to recall Mannheim's overall concern with the liberal objective of showing how persuasive reason can be in command of power. From this standpoint there is a certain unity between the alternative currents: if sociology of knowledge cannot serve as the organon for a synthetic and reconciling understanding of the direction and meaning of historical development, providing a scientific grasp of the situation confronting all parties, in which all parties will recognize themselves, then it can at least be a propaedeutic for scientific social theory, prophylactic against ideologies and promoting enlightenment.

Mannheim's work in this domain must be understood as an ingenious, conscientious, and determined pursuit of the hunch that the way through the crisis of liberal civilization must pass through and beyond the relativizing insights of fashionable cultural productions, including knowledge. He is thinking this problem through, with the help of his philosophical model of knowledge derived from phenomenological speculation and which he had elaborated in his essay on the structural analysis of epistemology. He emphasizes throughout a regulative ideal of philosophy of history, inspired above all by Hegelian readings of Marx, as well as the exemplary empiricism of outstanding sociological writers, especially Max Weber, whose achievements give him a professional reference point when his speculations threaten to make him over-dependent on the belletristic and pseudo-philosophical devices of the cultural essayists. And his thinking is conditioned by a strong sense of political responsibility, amid changing readings of the political situation.

It is Mannheim's paradoxical thesis, in the main current of his thought at this time, that ideologies count as knowledge by virtue of the very fact that is commonly used to discredit them. Precisely because they are each rooted in the perspective specific to some social group, they are authentically connected to the real processes of social existence and to the way in which knowledge arises and works within it. Each group, of course, sees different threats and possibilities in the situation and needs to know different things about it. That is why ideologies are perspectival. But each does know something, and knows it well. In his explication of such knowledge in *Structures of Thinking*, he speaks of 'conjunctive' knowledge, and means by this a knowledge 'in touch' with things and shareable only among knowers similarly situated and somehow in contact with one another (or among connoisseurs situated so as to develop a special sensibility for the historical variety of such knowledge).

In his work on conservatism, he elaborates a similar conception of a way of thinking attached to collective forms of life, in conjunction with his exposition of Savigny's conservative distinction between a law which is duly rooted in a communal sense of justice and a law which derives from juristic systematization. The term which Mannheim applies to the former is one of the two closely related terms for thinking bound up with existence which he uses throughout his subsequent work to characterize all social and political knowledge. The term is '*seinsverbundenes Denken*'. It is similar to '*seinsgebundenes Denken*'. Both expressions are more or less equivalent to thinking which is bound up with existence. In the English translation of *Ideologie und Utopie*, Mannheim approved 'existentially determined' as translation, in line with a general tendency toward rendering his concepts more like characterizations of empirically testable relationships. There is one passage in his 1931 handbook article on sociology of knowledge, not clear in the translation incorporated in *Ideology and Utopia*, where he distinguishes between the two terms. Enquiry into

'*Seinsverbundenheit*', he suggests, will help overcome '*Seinsgebundenheit*'. In this passage, he is quite evidently taking advantage of a nuance of difference between the two German expressions. They have different ranges of connotations. '*Verbundenheit*' extends to freely chosen and morally binding ties, while '*Gebundenheit*' reaches out towards compulsion. In that context, then, Mannheim is making the point that awareness of the social commitments constitutive of social knowledge will counter the mechanical and alienated forms of those commitments, operating as uncontrollable constaints. The distinction, in short, refers to a dimension of his argument which is different from the basic point that social knowledge is socially rooted knowledge, although it presupposes an attenuation of this point insofar as it applies to the distance between sociology of knowledge and social existence.[19]

But Mannheim's continuities with this conservative idea do not extend to the notion that only communities which are somehow bound by soil and tradition can possess such knowledge. In his initial formulations in *Structures of Thinking* of the distinction between 'conjunctive' and 'communicative' thinking, he does move along these lines, since he suggests that the latter type of thinking, the product of social modernization and rationalization, has tended to obliterate human meanings. In his later work on conservatism, however, he refers authentic social knowledge to the collective experiences of classes in complex industrial societies, and this takes his far from conservative praise of communal ways of thought. The positive connotation of existential rootedness, nevertheless, continues as an important characteristic in his thinking.

This criterion plays a key part in the distinction which Mannheim proposes in the first essay of *Ideologie und Utopie* between the 'partial' and the 'total' concepts of ideology. The former, he observes, derives from intellectualist distrust of purposive discourse, but nevertheless quite adequately comprehends the self-interested manipulative designs in political persuasion. But Mannheim is above all concerned with the authentic cultural phenomenon corresponding to the second of the concepts, in which a style of thought inherent in a social and historical location is meant. Total ideology constitutes a way of knowing. While an analyst employing the partial concept would uncover the interested motive underlying, for example, a newspaper editorial welcoming a certain measure of unemployment as an incentive to productivity, Mannheim would have investigated, as Gunnar Myrdal has done, the ideological context which gives meaning to such concepts as 'unemployment' and 'productivity' and the social and historical roots of this ideology. The latter analysis would not only lead to an appreciation of the powers and historical limitations of bourgeois political economy, according to Mannheim, but it would also bring into view the competing presence of what Marx called the 'political economy of the proletariat'. Study of the 'total ideology' opens the way to the ideological field and to the historical situation of which it is a part. Sociology of knowledge, on this reading, is concerned with establishing a vital connection to this underlying historical situation.

But the emphasis on the authenticity of ideological knowledge raises anew the question about the need for an integrative force, such as sociology of knowledge claims to be. If the clash and conflict among ideologies in an age of concentration and competition are tied to the social reality of the time, the process itself would seem to manifest the inner truth of this reality.

At times, indeed, Mannheim appears to suggest that the political process of competition itself is the locus of all the knowledge required for politics and that its inner mechanisms suffice to bring about and monitor the realism that is socially necessary. Along this line of speculation, he sees a certain similarity between politics and the liberal conception of parliament, which portrayed it as a forum for rational disputation and as an institutionalization of the mechanisms by which knowledge is tested and validated. After suggesting the similarity, however, he distinguishes his own understanding of the political forum from the liberal one by adapting from Marxism a conception of politics as a process of dialectical interplay among factors more 'real' than the contrasting rational judgements within a common methodological framework, which is all that liberalism, in his view, could comprehend. Unlike the Marxists he refuses to identify one of the 'real' political forces as the bearer of a transcendent rationality, historically destined to reintegrate all the struggling irrationalities within a higher, pacified order. The contesting social forces and their projects in the world appear to him as complementary and in need of a synthesis that will incorporate elements of their diverse social wills and visions.

The question remains, however, whether Mannheim's use of the term *Realdialektik* for the political process does not suggest that he considers it competent, over time, to make its own adjustments to the historical situation as it unfolds. It is tempting to speculate that one of the possibilities which Mannheim implicitly keeps open in this respect derives from the model of democratic politics developed at the time by the jurists Hans Kelsen and Ernst Fraenkel. Social-democratic in their political sympathies, they sought during the 1920s to counter the vision of a homogeneous and rational general will which went with revolutionary impatience on the left of their own party as well as to oppose the authoritarian disdain for pluralistic politics on their right. They portrayed democracy as an ongoing non-violent contestation among a plurality of collective interests, and attached more importance to civilizing the conduct of conflict and implementing the interim compromises reached from time to time than to projecting some transcendent outcome.[20]

Mannheim never acknowledges any of this literature. His only major reference to Kelsen is a critical aside in a methodological essay, where he cites him as a neo-Kantian unable to grasp the relationship between sociological and legal analyses. The fundamental difference with them, even during the few years when the partially coinciding conceptions appeared plausible, has to do with contrasting ways of thinking about the constitution of a civilized political process.

Mannheim does not think that such a political process could function without a contribution from thinking which transcends ideological perspectives, and sociology of knowledge, in his view, is needed to generate it. Legalism will not serve. Writing in the late 1920s, he depicts the ideological field as being in a state of 'crisis', which makes purely immanent dialectical development impossible. On the one hand, a number of the ideological contenders set forth their claims in terms so sweeping and absolute that they imply the annihilation of all opponents and make for acts of violence which are mindless and carry no promise of revolutionary transformation and reconstitution. On the other hand, all ideological contenders use the concept of ideology, in its purely destructive form, to disorient and discredit their opponents, thereby mutually undermining their confidence in their own understandings and aspirations. This opens another way to pointless violent direct action. The sociology of knowledge brings into being an experience of interdependence. It intervenes by demonstrating to each group the limitations on its own perspective, due to its dependence on a given location in social time and space, while also affirming the cognitive value of each perspective for comprehending a dimension of a complex situation.

There is thus an interesting parallel between the way in which theory of knowledge serves above all, according to the essay on the structural analysis of epistemology, to render many kinds of knowledge legitimate, even while restricting the scope of the claims of each, and the ways in which the sociology of knowledge is seen to function. Similar too is the expectation that this function would somehow flow into the constitution of a new state of knowledge, providing a new grounding for it, and thereby changing the ultimate state of things overall. More pertinently, though, the legitimating and constituting function of the sociology of knowledge is also analogous to the functions of the democratic constitutional and legal systems in Kelsen's juristic theory.

Both provide a civilizing framework which denies the universality of the claims put forward by competing political actors, while granting them some legitimacy as partisan participants in an unresolvable competition. But the differences between the two are very great and bear on a major issue in dispute during the Weimar years, the power of legality.

Mannheim's work skirts all around this dispute, from his use of Max Weber's sociology of law as paradigm for sociology of culture in his first treatment of the discipline,[21] to his exclusion of all but juristic writers from his study of conservatism, to his characterization finally of all forms of legalism as aspects of liberal indifference to the irrationalities of power and conflict. What Kelsen entrusts to the legal manifestation of the democratically organized sovereign state, Mannheim would put upon a basis of comprehensive, intercommunicated social knowledge about the common historical situation. For Mannheim, Kelsen exemplifies the 'idealist' attempt to generate a normative order without reference to the actual situation and to impose it upon social existence from 'above'. The normativizing activity of the sociology of knowledge, in contrast, he sees as rooted in the same cultural and political developments as the conflicts it is to regulate and the crisis it is to overcome. This gives it an authenticity and connectedness, in his view, which no legal structure can claim. It offers a genuine constitution.[22]

As if often the case at key points in Mannheim's argument, there is a paradox here. Like other forms of social knowledge, the synthetic achievement of the sociology of knowledge depends for its cognitive integrity on being rooted in the social reality which it explicates. Yet sociology of knowledge is said to be grounded in a social stratum comparatively detached from the parties contesting the social terrain. The question is whether the style of thought peculiar to intellectuals can be authentic or whether it is bound to be a superficial, surface phenomenon. In many of his essays, Mannheim accepts this paradox without comment, letting the literary familiarity with dialectical ironies carry the burden of the argument. In other places, however, he concedes the need to show his intellectuals as disciplined by constraints which his theory of their social location alone would not account for. His impatience with the superficial 'impressionism' of the sophisticated and relativist intellectuals and his distrust of the Romantic indiscipline of anti-rationalist literary intellectuals had been, after all, starting points for his own work. This distrust is echoed in his subsequent reading of fascism as the ideology of a stratum of intellectuals who are 'outsiders', as well as in his warning that an ideology and political course designed by intellectuals on their own behalf could only be a fascist one.[23] The intelligentsia, Mannheim observes,

> *is not a class and . . . it is therefore not in the position to form its own party.* Anyone who believes that a party of intellectuals is necessary has gotten the diagnosis of intellectuals wrong. It would be a complete accident if anything at all reasonable came of this. And that can hardly be the basis for gaining consciousness. Above all, it has to be recognized that there is no group that is as divided internally (bank director, professor, yellow journalist, bohemian), and that this division is a division according to classes. More than that: the formation of a party of intellectuals would inevitably lead to fascism.[24]

Nevertheless, he insists in the 1932 lecture from which this passage is taken, that intellectuals must follow the proletarian example as explained by Marxism. They must become aware of their distinctive mission by gaining consciousness of themselves as a group. Then they will exercise free choice in the construction of knowledge and in the selection of action. This paradox about authenticity and his ambivalence about intellectuals are clearly among the considerations which keep alive for Mannheim an alternative theory about the sociology of knowledge and its relationship to ideology, and bring the alternative very much to the fore when fascism gains its ascendancy, first in large circles of the academic and extramural intelligentsia and then, overwhelmingly, in the cultural domain as a whole.

From the standpoint of this second alternative the sociology of knowledge appears, above all, as a specialized subdivision of applied sociology, and the validity of its various findings and theories is referred to standards appropriate to this value-free discipline. While the emergence of the discipline may be accounted for by social theory, the integrity of its practitioners and the value of their work depend on their submission to its internal norms. This is reminiscent of Mannheim's intellectual world as it appears in 'Structural Analysis of Epistemology' and in other works prior to his projection of a philosophy of history as unifying ground for thought. It implies a pluralism of autonomous modes of knowledge, moreover, that renders more uncertain the cognitive role of the movement towards synthesis in the ideology-process, as that movement is envisioned by the design of sociology of knowledge as organon.

Ideology, in the more limited approach, appears as false consciousness, as a view of the world distorted by the effects of unconscious social compulsions. Even in the introductory essay of *Ideologie und Utopie*, Mannheim keeps open the possibility of associating his own concept with this negative connotation of the term. This is the conception contained in the 'evaluative' concept of ideology, which Mannheim distinguishes from a 'non-evaluative' one, since it is in the former frame of reference that ideology appears as something categorically different from knowledge. The 'non-evaluative' concept of ideology, in contrast, pertains to a conception of sociology of knowledge as a superior but complicitous collaborator in the ideological process. Mannheim at one time suggests a dialectical movement between these conceptions, taking them as appearing at successive levels of analysis, but he does not work out a persuasive statement of this presumed development, and the designs emerge as incompatible alternatives.

The conception of sociology of knowledge as discipline is much closer to Max Weber's categorical distinction between scientific words as ploughshares and political words as swords than is the conception of sociology of knowledge as organon. The continued attractiveness to Mannheim of the former possibility owes much to his unfinished business with Weber: his attraction to Weber's teachings about empiricism, rigour, and intellectual asceticism, which always coexists with his fascination with historicist and phenomenological approaches. Mannheim hopes to achieve a dialectical 'change in function' (*Funktionswechsel*) of Weber's social interpretation of culture, but he has no philosophical confidence in an Hegelian dialectical logic to serve that objective. In methodological reflections on that problem, he insists that the change could be achieved by the weight of evidence that Weber would have had to acknowledge. This consideration weighs against the attempt to ground comprehensive social knowledge on the historical and social identity of intellectuals. The focus shifts to a disciplinary structure embodied in the professional community of social scientists.

Mannheim's attempt to establish himself as a recognized member of the academic profession was thus a matter of principle as well as careerism. The popularity of such authors as Oswald Spengler and the disdain for them among the serious writers Mannheim respected, as well as the excited manifestos against Weber's scientific ethos by such young writers as Erich von Kahler, close to the Stefan-George-Circle, and the avuncular condescension accorded that kind of criticism to Ernst Troeltsch, for example, made it important for Mannheim to choose sides.[25] When Mannheim turns from philosophy to sociology in the early 1920s, he first stakes out a position for himself on the boundary between the two disciplines. And as philosophical commentator on sociology, he criticizes the method of Weber and other empirical sociologists, especially with regard to cultural sociology. But in his surveys of possibilities in the field, he always treats the approaches he criticizes with respect, never challenging the scientific ethos Weber had struggled to establish in the profession.

Mannheim's *Conservatism* exemplifies an acceptance of strictly professional norms, during the same years when other essays laid out the possibilities of philosophy of history and social ontology. Subtitled 'a contribution to the sociology of knowledge', the work avoids speculation about the wider philosophical implications of its findings and presents itself, especially in the shortened version which Mannheim published, as simply an empirical study of the social conditions under which the conservative style of thinking arose and changed. The professional factor naturally weighs even more heavily after Mannheim succeeds Franz Oppenheimer as Professor of Sociology at Frankfurt and takes over his predecessor's course in historical sociology.

In addition to those lectures, his primary interest at Frankfurt is a postgraduate seminar on the social and intellectual history of early German liberalism, which was intended, according to one of its participants, to be 'an empirically oriented . . . interdisciplinary project, similar to his earlier empirical work on "das konservative Denken" '. The siminar, given jointly with the young economist Adolfe Löwe and some others, addressed itself to questions about modern and classical liberal economics as well as to more general political themes. In September 1934, Mannheim and Löwe jointly presented a five-day seminar in the Netherlands on 'Economy and Man in the Age of Planning'. The notice of the event states that they are 'long accustomed to scientific collaboration with one another', and, indeed, the printed articles which are, by internal evidence, the outgrowth of the contribution of each, attest to mutual indebtedness and agreement.

Löwe's elaboration appears in *Economics and Sociology*, also given as lectures in 1935 at the London School of Economics. Strikingly, he opens the lecture with a vehement attack on the 'popular prejudice' that sociological method consists of 'interpretation based on inner understanding and comparative description, but not causal analysis'. German sociology, he observes, has distracted itself too long with unproductive self-reflections and worries about differing modes of knowledge. Causal explanations based on empirical evidence are the goal in the social sciences, as in any other, and intepretive methods are nothing more than suggestive aids in generating hypotheses and first approximations, to give direction to work which is properly scientific in character. His talk ends with the claim that 'the main field and true justification' of the sociology of knowledge, professed above all by Karl Mannheim in his handbook article on the sociology of knowledge, is to contrast the 'obscure fallacies and prejudices' of common sense with the 'scientific results of the competent specialism'.[26]

The close collaboration between Mannheim and Löwe testifies to Mannheim's adaptability to various collaborators and audiences as well as to a shift in his position in the course of the 1930s. Mannheim never opted definitively for the position espoused by Löwe, and he certainly had not done so during the years before he left Germany. Evidence concerning the composition of the very article which Löwe cites is revealing about Mannheim's continued play with multiple possibilities. Portions of a preliminary draft found in Mannheim's files are considerably more 'phenomenological' and oriented to social ontology than his account of the sociology of knowledge as it was published in the professional handbook, and the conception of sociology of knowledge as mediator in the ideology-process rather than as disinterested specialized discipline is much more in evidence.[27] Löwe's suggestion that he and Mannheim shared common ground builds quite properly on one of Mannheim's experimental postures and indicates one of Mannheim's sources of support and encouragement in this direction, but it treats as settled a complex of matters that Mannheim never resolved.

Where Mannheim does attempt to press the case for the distinctive intellectual structure of social knowledge and to distinguish his own approach from that of Max Weber, he puts special emphasis on the admixture of rational calculability and 'irrational' volitions in the concepts and logical design of all such knowledge, as well as on the historicity and partiality of what is discernible from even the most synoptic and comprehensive perspective. He argues, for example, that a concept like 'capitalism' gains its analytical and even its descriptive force, notwithstanding its specifiable empirical referent, from a socially rooted design to comprehend human relationships by reference to different and transitory modes of property, in order to change those modes. The concept is ultimately 'at home' within socialist ideology. The availability and bearing of the concept, moreover, depend on a certain historical constellation of factors; when this changes, he suggests, it will make little sense to apply this term, even where conduct in the sphere which has been called economic appears identical.

Mannheim denies that such analysis involves relativist undermining of its own claims because the analysis works out of the structure of knowledge appropriate to the reality towards which it is directed and pertinent to the attitudes which shape knowing in this domain. The contrast model of universally valid knowledge which is essential to the meaning of relativism, he maintains, simply has no relevance. Even where Mannheim is less sanguine about his larger claims, he insists on the propriety of recording the perspectivism and historicity of social knowledge in social science, maintaining that he is simply registering patterns empirically present in that knowledge and that he is content to leave questions about the philosophical ramifications of these findings to practitioners of the discipline of philosophy. It is, accordingly, not so much the problem of relativism that makes Mannheim uneasy about the distinctive structure he proposes for social knowledge as it is his resistance to the hyper-activist fascist threat to rationality of any kind.

Mannheim's position concerning the ineradicable volitional component in social thinking, originally formulated as part of an attack upon positivist or neo-Kantian stringencies concerning the logic of epistemologically justifiable enquiry, becomes defensive when challenged by the contention which Mannheim repeatedly summed up in the irrationalist slogan, 'Willing the right thing makes for valid knowledge'.[28] Mannheim had always attempted to distance himself from such an irrationalist extension of the existentialist phenomenology which intrigued him and which stimulated his formulation of the approach associated with sociology of knowledge as organon. Accordingly, he had always insisted that the knowledge he was seeking could be articulated in orderly forms whose logic could be extrapolated and applied critically to appropriate knowledge claims in the same domain, even if comprehension might require a receptivity which is existentially grounded and not

universally accessible. Confronted now with assertions that
ideologies expressing a national or racial will to power are immune
to challenge and sufficiently vindicated by the achievement of
power, however, the sufficiency of his own more rational criteria
seem unclear.

He then insists on the great difference between a view which
vaunts its volitionalist irrationality and one which only gives in to
the need to acknowledge a residue of social design in all social
knowledge, after having struggled to eliminate all possible vestiges
of volition from its structure. From this point of view the volitional
element no longer appears as a cognitive asset to Mannheim. This
shift to a more defensive posture with regard to a notion central to
the very idea of sociology of knowledge as organon implies a change
not only in its methodological aspirations, bringing them much
closer to the ideals of empirical social science, but also in its functions.

For Mannheim, knowledge always serves to provide 'orientation' for the knower with regard to the domain which is known and
with reference to the search for direction which the knower brings to
the activity of knowing. In the conception of sociology of knowledge
as the way to a synthesis of social knowledge, the orientation is
thought to refer to the political domain as such, where competing
social visions grounded in different social designs struggle with one
another in the attempt to bring the future into being. Orientation, in
this conception, lays the basis for mediation to break the impasse of
mutual discrediting among ideologies. It promises to obviate the
pointless violence symptomatic of this crisis. Knowledge illuminates
the 'situation' and makes possible the 'next step'.

Mannheim actually entertains two very different kinds of
doubts about this conception of the function of sociology of knowledge. The first, worked out in the essay on utopian thought in
Ideologie und Utopie, points in quite the opposite direction from the
one formative for much of his later work. In that essay, he reconcep-
tualizes the volitional, driving force in 'ideologies', speaking of it as
the 'utopian' component which carries a demand for change. Such
utopianism, he speculates, is being dispelled by a new realism fostered by the social sciences, and the paradoxical prospect emerges
that humankind will cease to have any impulse to action and thus
also to knowledge just as it has finally gained the capacity to make
its own history. This vision contrasts sharply with the picture of
dynamic political contestation portrayed in Mannheim's other
major essays in *Ideologie und Utopie* and in the other writings of the

time. Mannheim wrote the essay as a tribute to Alfred Weber and used the occasion to experiment once again with a kind of cultural criticism which he had largely left behind after his earliest Hungarian writings, a confrontation between an over-rationalized, weary world and the impossibility of the imperative radical renewal. Whether Mannheim's experiment was conditioned by the literary occasion or by the political circumstances of 1928, when political imagination seems really to have flagged very badly in Weimar Germany, the work illustrates dramatically Mannheim's willingness to work from various sets of premises and his extraordinary talent for making his exercises yield interesting results.

But the concern with hyper-rationalization, in anything like this form, was not to be his real topic during the next years. The successful National Socialist movement, it might be said, cruelly parodied the function which Mannheim had designed for the synthetic science of politics: it provided a comprehensive *Weltanschauung* which gave millions a sense of having regained orientation, and it effectively dissolved the ideological impasse. Mannheim suddenly found that the ideologically informed political contestation, in which sociology of knowledge was to intervene transformatively, was being replaced by cultural and political forms in which great masses were swept by emotions to accept barbarously misleading but uniform myths about social realities and prospects. Under such conditions, the notion of sociology of knowledge as an organon for a science of politics appears irrelevant. It can serve, at most, as an aid to thinkers trying to stay free of the tide and attempting, with the help of insight into the compulsions at work within themselves as well, to gain a clear understanding of what is happening.

In Mannheim's lectures in Frankfurt in 1931 and 1932, he outlined an approach to the study of sociology which, he claims, reveals it to be a *lebenswissenschaftliche Methode*, a science for living. The knowledge of everyday life, he insists, is wholly misleading, distorted by mythologies which render individuals unable to comprehend their situations or to act appropriately in them. This represents a radical break with the line of thinking which had generated the view of sociology of knowledge as organon, since that line followed Dilthey in distinguishing between the specialized knowledge achievable by scientific disciplines and the range and richness available to the 'whole man', to the actor in political situations but also in everyday life. Mannheim is moving here towards a stark contrast between scientifically grounded social knowledge and all other opinion.

The impact of fascism on Mannheim's thinking about the sociology of knowledge reveals the central premise on which the possibility of sociology of knowledge as organon for a science of politics had rested. If the way to comprehensive understanding of the 'situation' and an appreciation of its place in an historical process with some meaning and direction can be thought to occur by way of an encounter with the ideologies in the field, uncovering their groundedness but also their limitations by finding their place in the larger historical context, then it must be because those ideologies are somehow valid embodiments of the human spirit whose composite effort gives meaning to things. Once Mannheim decided that the conduct of everyday life is oriented by destructive delusions, at least in certain historical epochs, then the vocation of the seeker for knowledge once more appears simply and perhaps hopelessly as the task of Enlightenment.

The concept of Enlightenment returns to an important place in Mannheim's thinking. In the Frankfurt lectures on the approach to sociology, he speaks of the discipline as a method for shedding light on oneself and on one's situation. But in order to have access to sociological knowledge, he maintains, it is first necessary to have experienced the anomalies and paradoxes of social life. He speaks of women who have education but empty roles, intellectuals who are cultivated but without any influence, young people who are competent but unemployed. In general, he emphasizes the experience of being blocked from any possibility of social advancement. Sociology, then, is designed to enable the person to become aware of his location and social identity and then to comprehend the situation. Sociology of knowledge may have a part to play in this process, but it clearly can no longer constitute a new synthesis.

Mannheim's loss of confidence in the notion of sociology of knowledge as organon did not lead him to abandon the design for a science of politics. In his late German writings, before his exile, the conception of a diagnostic structural analysis is a recurrent theme. Later, in the English writings, this is combined with a stress on finding social techniques to counter the socially disruptive irrationalities which his socio-analysis had revealed to him.

NOTES

[1]   *Man and Society in an Age of Reconstruction* (London: Routledge & Kegan Paul, 1940), p. 33.

[2] Letter of January 5, 1912, 'Karl Mannheim's Letters to Lukács, 1910–1916', *The New Hungarian Quarterly*, Vol. XVI, No. 57 (Spring 1971), p. 98.

[3] See Mannheim's review of Lukács's book in *Logos* **9** (1920–2), pp. 298–302. Reprinted in Karl Mannheim *Wissenssoziologie*, Kurt H. Wolff, ed. (Berlin and Neuwied: Luchterhand, 1964), pp. 85–90. The context of Mannheim's review is a special issue devoted to critiques of Spengler. The journal as a whole helped to define the issues and approaches that Mannheim found most salient. In his 1917 lecture ('Soul and Culture'), Mannheim cites as models for himself and for others in his 'generation' Dostoyevsky, Kierkegaard, the German periodical *Logos*, the Hungarian periodical *Szellem*, the philosophers Lask and Zalai, the art historians Ernst and Riegl, Cézanne, and the *Nouvelle Revue Française*.

[4] On Georg Lukács and the 'Sunday Circle' see Éva Gábor, 'Mannheim in Hungary and in Weimar Germany', *Newsletter* of the *International Society for the Sociology of Knowledge*, **9**, 1&2 (August 1983), p. 7.

[5] See Lee Congdon, *The Young Lukács* (Chapel Hill and London: The University of North Carolina Press, 1983), p. 175. See also Éva Gábor, *op. cit.*, p. 8.

[6] Letter from Heidelberg, *Tüz* (Vienna), *1*, 1921, pp. 46–50.

[7] *Ibid.*

[8] *Ibid.*

[9] *Structures of Thinking*, ed. D. Kettler, V. Meja and N. Stehr (London: Routledge & Kegan Paul, 1982), pp. 31–139.

[10] *Ibid.*, pp. 141–288.

[11] The published version is 'Das konservative Denken', *Archiv für Sozialwissenschaft und Sozialpolitik* **57**, 1(1927): 68–142; 2: 470–95. English: 'Conservative Thought', in *Essays on Sociology and Social Psychology* (London: Routledge & Kegan Paul, 1953), pp. 74–164. The title of the *Habilitationsschrift* is *Altkonservatismus: Ein Beitrag zur Soziologie des Wissens*. The full text will be published in German and English: *Konservatismus*, ed. David Kettler, Volker Meja and Nico Stehr (Frankfurt: Suhrkamp, 1984); *Conservatism* (London and Henley: Routledge & Kegan Paul, 1985).

[12] 'Die Strukturanalyse der Erkenntnistheorie', *Kant-Studien*, Supplement 57 (Berlin: Reuther und Reichard, 1922). English: 'Structural Analysis of Epistemology', in *Essays on Sociology and Social Psychology*, ed. Paul Kecskemeti (London: Rout-

ledge & Kegan Paul, 1953), pp. 15–73.

[13]   'Historismus', *Archiv für Sozialwissenschaft und Sozialpolitik* **52**, 1
       (1924), pp. 1–60. Reprinted in Karl Mannheim, *Wissens-
       soziologie*, ed. Kurt H. Wolff, p. 263. English: 'Historicism', in
       Essays on the Sociology of Knowledge, pp. 84–133.

[14]   In *Wissenssoziologie*, ed. Kurt H. Wolff (Neuwied: Luch-
       terhand, 1964), p. 138.

[15]   Karl Mannheim, 'Die Strukturanalyse der Erkenntnis-
       theorie', in Wissenssoziologie, p. 172.

[16]   See Max Weber, 'Wissenschaft als Beruf', in *Wissenschaftslehre*
       (Tübingen: J. C. B. Mohr (Paul Siebeck), 1922), p. 613 and
       Karl Mannheim, *Ideologie und Utopie*, p. 143.

[17]   In Volker Meja and Nico Stehr, eds., *Der Streit um die Wissens-
       soziologie*, Vol. 1 (Frankfurt: Suhrkamp, 1982), pp. 325–370.
       English: 'Competition as a Cultural Phenomenon', Kurt H.
       Wolff, ed., *From Karl Mannheim* (London, Oxford University
       Press, 1971) pp. 223–261.

[18]   *Die Gegenwartsaufgaben der Soziologie* (Tübingen: J. C. B. Mohr
       (Paul Siebeck), 1932), p. 38. See also his claim, in the *Encyc-
       lopaedia of the Social Sciences* Vol. 15 (1935) entry on Toennies,
       that the Weimar Republic had been distinguished by the fact
       that it recognized the value of sociology for the training of
       citizens, which was Mannheim's primary teaching at the time
       he wrote that entry.

[19]   The English version of *Ideology and Utopia* omits the distinction
       between Seins*verbundenheit* and Seins*gebundenheit* altogether,
       rendering them both as 'situational determination'. See A. P.
       Simonds, *Karl Mannheim's Sociology of Knowledge* (Oxford:
       Clarendon Press, 1978), p. 27, and Volker Meja, 'The Sociol-
       ogy of Knowledge and the Critique of Ideology', *Cultural Her-
       meneutics* **3** (1975), p. 67n.

[20]   See on this also Wolfgang Luthardt's essay on 'Politik-
       theoretische Aspekte im Werk von Hans Kelsen', in Richard
       Saage, ed., *Politische Konzeptionen der Sozialdemokratie zwischen
       den Weltkriegen* (Frankfurt: Suhrkamp, 1984).

[21]   *Structures of Thinking*, pp. 60–63.

[22]   For the sense of 'constitution' employed here, cf. Kenneth
       Burke, *A Grammar of Motives* (New York: Prentice-Hall, 1945),
       pp. 341f.

[23]   See 'Ist Politik als Wissensschaft möglich?', in *Ideologie und
       Utopie*, p. 123.

[24]   Cf. the report on Mannheim's Amsterdam lecture on 'Die

soziale und politische Bedeutung der Intelligenz': H. v. W., 'De Sociologie der Intellektuellen', *Propria Cures* (Amsterdam), **44**, 7 (October 29, 1932).

[25] See, for example, the special issue of *Logos*, *op. cit.*, devoted to refutations of Spengler, as well as Troeltsch's 'Die Revolution in der Wissenschaft' (1921), in *Aufsätze zur Geistesgeschichte und Religionssoziologie* (Tübingen: J. C. B. Mohr (Paul Siebeck), 1925).

[26] The account of the Frankfurt seminar is from a letter by W. Baldamus, 22 November 1979; see also the preface by Ulrich Hermann to Hans H. Gerth's book, *Bürgerliche Intelligenz um 1800: Zur Soziologie des deutschen Frühliberalismus* (Göttingen: Vandenhoeck & Ruprecht, 1976), p. 9. The quotation is from Löwe's *Economics and Sociology* (London: George Allen & Unwin, 1935), pp. 33, 152 and 152 n. 1.

[27] 'Wissenssoziologie', *Handwörterbuch der Soziologie*, ed. Alfred Vierkandt (Stuttgart: Enke, 1931), pp. 659–80. Translated by Louis Wirth and Edward Shils in *Ideology and Utopia*, pp. 237–80. The preliminary draft is among the Mannheim papers at the University of Keele, England.

[28] The German is 'Wahres Wollen fundiert wahres Wissen'. One place where Mannheim rejects such a reading of his position on ideology is *Die Gegenwartsaufgaben der Soziologie* (The Tasks of Sociology Called for by the Present), which is in general an important source for Mannheim's professional reconsideration of his more experimental writings, clearly written in the light of the political situation in 1932 and his sense of his responsibility to sociology as a discipline still in search of legitimacy, especially in the judgement of the educators to whom the overview was delivered.

3

Diagnostic Sociology

THERAPEUTIC SOCIAL PSYCHOLOGY

As the sociology of knowledge ceased to play a leading methodological part in his thinking, Mannheim turned more frequently to medical imagery to characterize his intellectual activities. In a note for his files, he lists himself along with a number of social thinkers and movements, including Freud, Durkheim, Ortega y Gasset, Max and Alfred Weber, and John Dewey, under the key words, 'Diagnostic Sociology, Diagnosis, eine Prognosis, eine Cure, Education'.[1] No longer simply an interpreter and mediator who helps to orient politically creative actors and fosters the tendencies towards synthesis, the social thinker is to become a socio-therapist, who clinically analyses social disorders, devises therapeutic regimens, and overcomes the inhibitions and distortions which hinder remedial action.

In a lecture, given in September 1933 in the Netherlands and reacting to the shock of political events and personal exile, Mannheim introduces the conception of 'socio-analysis' as a way of coping with the massive irrationalities symptomized by the Nazi triumph.

> This should be viewed as a complement to psychoanalysis. While the latter breaks the whole terrain of phenomena down into factors which it then studies, socio-analysis, in

contrast, attempts to uncover the connection between phenomena and their contexts, the structure of the situation. Its objective is education as well as therapy, especially with regard to social pathologies. It seeks to achieve this by analysis and illumination of the situation. While psychoanalysis penetrates to the un- and sub-conscious, socio-analysis is concerned with the semi-conscious, where there are also processes under way which have great effect on the persons affected.[2]

This conception of socio-analysis, with its implicit distinction between pathological and healthy states of man and society, brings to a head Mannheim's growing conviction that ordinary thinking has proved itself incapable of providing orientation in the contemporary situation and that some mode of extraordinary, methodically acquired knowledge is needed to provide enlightenment and to restore rationality to social conduct. With this appears the clearly evident need to judge events by a standard more discriminating than historical success or the people's sense of union in dynamic movement. Mannheim moves closer to the liberal appeal to reason and to liberal standards of individual personality and responsibility. In a manner more reminiscent of Durkheim than Max Weber, however, he treats these liberal themes as *sociological* problems and *collective* tasks. And, in express continuity with Freud, he finds a therapeutic application for the knowledge acquired.

In their Dutch collaboration, while Löwe lectured on 'the reconstruction of the economy', Mannheim projected 'the reconstruction of man'.[3] This ambitious objective, moreover, introduces a certain dualism into his theory. Mannheim asks not only about the individualizing forces in society which may be therapeutically enlisted against the sway of 'mass-man', but also about the extent to which the desires of 'mass-man' can be re-formed by propaganda. In moving toward his new emphasis on 'planning', Mannheim shifts from a conception of knowledge with a largely catalytic function towards a knowledge which is more instrumental for purposes of control. This knowledge cannot be thought simply to inform a revitalized political process; it belongs to a planning elite and it must be consciously and continuously wielded by them. The healing of society, it now seems, requires supersession of politics by a new mode of coordinating human conduct in spheres as yet unrationalized, a mode that will dispense with conflict and competition. Mannheim now shows little confidence in the recuperative powers of the social process, as it has functioned in history. 'Reconstruction', accordingly, involves a way of knowing that will show how to manipulate present-day populations as well as how to transform them into more rational actors.[4]

Mannheim characterizes this knowledge with the help of an evolutionary scheme. Reflecting the interplay between himself and Löwe in the formation of this new approach, he takes Adam Smith's economic theory as a model of the highest achievement of what he calls 'thought at the level of invention', a stage intermediate between 'thought at the level of chance discovery' and 'thought at the level of planning'. Smith, Mannheim maintains, abstracts an autonomous cycle of causes from the complexity of historical social life and subsumes each of the elements to principles of the highest generality. This type of thinking, he claims, is appropriate to a stage of historical development in which rational conduct involves mastery of the different internal requirements of diverse subsystems comprising social life, including subsystems subjected to very little rationalization. The whole system is integrated by more or less automatic social processes.

An increased 'density' of social happenings makes the dimensions interdependent at decisive points and renders this way of thinking anachronistic, Mannheim contends. So, for example, economic processes are profoundly affected by political ones, as when workers demand 'political wages', industry organizes around governmentally supported combinations, and the psychology of social expectations undergoes changes which render the assumptions of *ceteris paribus* in classical economics altogether unrealistic. Correspondingly, according to Mannheim, the controls exercised within any of these subsystems have the most profound consequences upon events assigned to another subsystem by the older thinking. The leaders of major trade union organizations or the directors of the enormous industrial combinations, for example, control institutions whose actions can render the decisions and designs of government irrelevant. If thinking is to perform its proper function of expanding the 'radius of foresight' to the full extent of the 'radius of action', so that actors can understand the entire range of consequences directly traceable to their actions and can take responsibility for them, it is necessary to develop a way of thinking that will comprehend interdependencies.

The situation in Weimar Germany can illustrate Mannheim's method. There were relationships among borrowing, capital formation, investment, wages, and prices with consequences projectable by economic analysis; transformations in the character and uses of law analysable by jurists; patterns of interest group alliance and contestation comprehensible to political science, shifts in structures of political belief and loyalty of concern to political sociologists; and changes in the social organization of cultural life best explained by cultural sociologists. Out of this complex of factors arose novel forms of mass political movements which cannot be understood without the tools of social psychology. There was a movement in Germany towards a proletarian revolution; there was a tendency towards regroupment of rational social forces imbued with a new realism; and there was a tendency towards fascist exploitation of mass disorientation, social uncertainty and intense will among minorities with nothing to lose.

Mannheim claims that 'planning' involves a distinctive way of grasping what he calls the *'principia media'*, i.e., the interacting causes that constitute the 'situation' which conditions the effects of any individual causal chain analytically identified or practically set in motion. That cluster of causes, comprising elements which are likely to be the specialized subject matter of quite different sciences, cannot be read unequivocally, since it is so complex and since the interaction of factors may invoke new elements in turn. 'Planning', then, is a matter of discerning 'trends', and there are likely to be multiple and opposing trends at work within a given situation. Narrative history also looks at a multiplicity of factors and possible outcomes, but 'thought at the level of planning' is far more instructive. Instead of an epic drama in which individual actors struggle with one another within a *mise en scène*, as in narrative history, it discerns a structure of alternative emerging possibilities and comprehends the variables determining the relative probabilities among them.

Mannheim links the mode of thinking that can read *principia media* to planning because he treats all knowledge as a function of conduct, and views this mode of knowing as incident to the new social capabilities for strategic interventions in situations. Such capabilities already exist, but they are misunderstood and misapplied. In the last years of Weimar, for example, government and business followed orthodox economic policies, expecting natural social forces to adjust the economic subsystem. They persisted in specialized thinking, along lines of separate social subsystems. They failed to realize that their actions would have profound consequences upon other social processes and that these would react so as to preclude the adjustments expected.

The occupants of key positions made choices based on obsolete thinking. They failed to recognize that the institutions they were controlling now intersected directly with patterns of cultural, psychological, and political development, and that the policies they implemented consequently had direct effects within numerous other spheres. An economically orthodox decision to close factories, for example, made by the management of huge concentrated industries dependent on the state for maintenance of its supplies and markets, represented a direct challenge to the trade unions associated with them in the corporate group process and a welcome opportunity for the communist and fascist competitors of those organizations. No economic theory can, as such, comprehend the interplay of forces in post-liberal society. In the event, Mannheim notes, such effects rendered the designs of key actors altogether vain and made possible the triumph of a crude but, under the circumstances, strategically effective plan of total social conquest, which was ruthlessly pursued by the outsider groups uniquely aware of the opportunities.

Mannheim was convinced that the Nazis won power in 1933 because they had planned and because they had recognized the power to be derived from a 'group strategy' based on social psychology. An alternative to their domination requires effective competition for those intellectual resources. Social psychology is so essential for grasping the *principia media* of the present age because the situation is defined, above all, by the unexpected breakdown of structures of rationality, the explosive eruption of mass irrationalities in a setting of social indecisiveness. No design for economic planning can proceed without intermeshing with the present state of group-expectations and motivations. Reconstructing the economy requires reconstructing the human actors who are to operate it, and this requires planful therapeutic engagement with them, in their social identities and locations.

There is no way out, Mannheim believes: people are bound to be planned in a world where there is too little social space for learning by trial and error, too little distance for spontaneity, too much crowding among masses and events. The question is only whether they will be planned for irrational feelings, mindless obedience, and destructive actions, or whether it will prove possible to put a collective social capacity for realistic judgement and measured conduct in place of the individualized rationalities which are forever gone.

In discussing the achievability of such planning, Mannheim returns to the expositional device familiar from his earlier work. He presents the design he is propounding as implicit in the work of many contemporaries. He claims for himself the vision to see what they are about:

> Apart from the cloistered systems of philosophy which merely sum up the results of past ages, there has always been another type, that of the pioneer who produced principles which at the next stage of social development were to become important tools of research, and set up the frame of reference into which specialists were later to insert for details. Seeking to follow this example, it seems to be our task to pick out the factors unconsciously at work in the empirical researches now under way, i.e., to demonstrate that in the scattered and apparently isolated philosophical, psychological, and educational tendencies of recent years, the will to plan is everywhere at work, though in most cases it has yet to become conscious.[5]

The three intellectual tendencies which Mannheim reviews are pragmatism, behaviourism, and psychoanalysis. He concludes that pragmatism has good insight into the inner connection between thought and action, but fails to appreciate fully the varied social forms of action to which thinking may pertain. Accordingly, he maintains, pragmatism does not understand the kind of thinking involved in planning. Such thinking is carried on by representative thinkers in conjunction with the ensemble of actions being performed by groups exercising the full variety of social functions. In other words, Mannheim asserts that the most useful thinking may be far removed from the self-understanding of individual actors carrying out their discrete tasks in the complex division of labour. Indeed, in his view, it must be so, if it is to be comprehensive and grasp the effects of the entire range of the interdependent activities.

It is in this connection, then, that Mannheim recalls the therapeutic conception of sociology of knowledge; but he adds remarkable new claims about the transformation to be achieved by the transcendence of thinking constrained by limited social locations:

> [Comprehensive thinking] only becomes possible if a new type of self-observation corresponding to the level of planning is developed. This new attitude consists in the fact that . . . the individual is able to perceive not only all the relevant facts and all the relevant ways of looking at things

(ultimately he must perceive them if he is to avoid destruction), but he also becomes capable of seeing his special position in the social process, and of understanding that his thought is shaped by his position. New possibilities of planning now arise which hitherto were difficult to conceive, even theoretically. The individual not only attains a knowledge of himself but he can learn to understand the factors that determine his conduct, and can thus even attempt to regulate them . . . . His understanding still remains a product of the historical process which arose independently of him. But through his understanding of this determination the individual for the first time raises himself above the historical process – which now, more than ever before, becomes subject to his own power.[6]

It is hard to assess such utopian projections, since much is left unclear. Is this omniscience and omnipotence, for example, to belong to an elite of reflective thinkers and planners, equally to all individuals, or to the human race as collectivity? The passage should be read as rhetorical invocation of the ancient vision of reason commanding the world of accident and change, revealing the memories and aspirations Mannheim means to enlist in his case for social reconstruction. He is using the conception of sociology of knowledge, originally shaped by recognition that the self-certainties of Enlightenment rationalism could not be sustained, to help imagine just such overmastering consciousness. The intellectual exercises, he had earlier proposed as a method for entering into the reason which his regulative ideal projected as immanent in history, now appear as a way to rational transcendence of history. But it may be misleading to characterize Mannheim's new rhetorical turns in the language of philosophical idealism. More to the point is the Baconian conception of a state of mind which has overcome the 'idols' obstructing knowledge and is prepared to employ the correct scientific method: 'planning' and not the sociology of knowledge now is to serve as 'organon'. In any case, the strategies for planned change which he actually proposes in countering the irrationalities of the time depend much less on total transformations of consciousness than they do on the applications of recent psychological theory, modified so as to render it more nearly a 'social' psychology.

Mannheim treats behaviorism with great ambivalence. While he criticizes its indifference to all the aspects of human personality which can only be grasped by 'sympathetic understanding', he recognizes its power over 'external individual behaviour'. He finds that fascist successes depend on such knowledge and he indicates that planning for the masses produced by the disintegration of the old social order must in any case begin with mastery of this type.

Psychoanalysis, in contrast, provides the contemporary tendency, according to Mannheim, which can be developed into the knowledge required to complete the human transformation required for the age of planning. It probes deeply enough to get at the structure of personality itself, although it betrays its liberal individualist origins by its indifference to social constituents of identity. Mannheim finds the work of Erich Fromm and Karen Horney indicative of the possibilities for incorporating more social awareness into the approach and he envisions a kind of depth-educational work to create the pioneers needed to establish the new social design. In this context, he calls for a reassessment of the achievements of the Enlightenment. What is often dismissed as a naive confidence in 'reason', he now maintains, is better understood as an original and pathbreaking effort to create a 'new social economy in the control of impulses and a new self-conscious guidance of the restraints which are still necessary'.[7] But these thinkers can only be respected as precursors of the effort now under way among the more socially aware psychoanalysts and in 'the subtler forms of pragmatism, like that of Dewey'.[8] The whole intellectual development must be understood as unsettled and barely cognizant of the new comprehensive functions needed.

Mannheim recognizes that behaviorism and psychoanalysis involve radically different scientific methods, theoretical doctrines, and modes of practical application, but he insists that these differences are not decisive:

Here we can be helped only by interdependent action and thought which make use of both the internal and external approaches in the sense that they combine at every step the transformation of society with the transformation of individual personality. Moreover, as with most theoretical paradoxes, the problem is insoluble [merely?] on the level of abstract thinking. The exaggerated consistency of one-sided logical systems of thought tears out of their context things which, if reconciled in action, can be gradually united into a more and more appropriate pattern of conduct. The solution of these theoretical paradoxes is always possible in practice if the carefully thought-out alternatives

are used not as final formulae, but as signposts to indicate
the possible trends of events.[9]

Pragmatism, behaviorism, and psychoanalysis, in short, appear as
alternative approximations to the planning appropriate to the present human situation, and they lend themselves to theoretical elaboration and practical experimentation in the struggle against both
irrational disruption and its brutal totalitarian social nemesis.

The actual structure of 'planning', taken as a mode of thinking,
is thus left quite uncertain. Despite his characterization of specialized scientific disciplines as products of 'thought at the level of
invention', Mannheim leaves planning very much dependent on
these sciences. What is involved, he says, is some distinctive way of
interrelating the lines of analysis generated by the sciences, some
way of grasping actual trends concretely under way in the situations
within which action is required. Overall, the proposal remains programmatic. A method of approach must be developed, he asserts,

a scientific technique for describing the developing historical process must be worked out. This technique should
serve those who are trying to discover existing trends and
who are determined to deal with future events in terms of
open alternatives, i.e., to approach ambiguous facts with
an open mind.[10]

RESTORING RATIONALITY

Mannheim's attempt to characterize this new way of thinking testifies to the continuities as well as to the changes in his conceptions.
Especially striking, in view of the initial thesis of the present
interpretation, is Mannheim's citation of John Stuart Mill's *Logic of
the Moral Sciences* as a source of ideas for interrelating the requirements of scientific theory and political practice, universality and
history, knowledge and character formation.

But Mannheim appears more taken with Mill's objectives than
with his actual intellectual strategies. Like Mannheim, Mill sought
for a 'science of human natue in the concrete, and for practical
purposes', 'the immediate . . . laws according to which social states
generate one another as society advances',[11] and 'the general scientific theory of the art, from which its practical methods will follow
as corollaries'.[12] His conceptions about the formation of theories
in the moral sciences, however, including the 'intermediate princi-

ples' which Mannheim cites, are far from the methods which Mannheim outlines. Mannheim's citation of Mill evinces affinities to
Mill's liberal themes of freedom, development of personality, and
responsible choice, but it does not signal adhesion to his philosophy
of science.

To account for knowledge of *principia media*, Mannheim retains
from his earlier thinking the idea that the model for adequate practical understanding is thinking 'in terms of situations as wholes', and
he recalls his earlier use of humanist notions in his elaboration of
this concept:

> The distinction between the accumulation of factual know-
> ledge and the capacity for independent judgement, be-
> tween the mere arrangement of details and their interpreta-
> tion in terms of a situation has long been clear in everyday
> life. This distinction is now becoming the concern of the
> theorists. A new type of scientific accuracy has taken the
> problem in hand. At the level of planned thinking, it is for
> the first time really scientifically possible to 'grasp a situa-
> tion', to be 'master of a situation', as the common sense
> expression puts it.[13]

The repeated invocation of 'science' makes it clear that Mannheim has abandoned his earlier differentiation between science and
social knowledge, as different in structure, ontological base, and
function. But the correlative emphasis on 'situation' indicates the
desire to maintain some distance between himself and ordinary
forms of positivism, to maintain the link between the knowledge in
question and responsible, rational acts of judgement. There is
nothing like this in Mill's methodology. In principle, at least, the
importance assigned to 'everyday life' and 'common sense knowledge' recalls and promises an egalitarian possibility, beyond the
sharp division between elite and mass required by the crisis of the
times. That is a connection, in the last analysis, between the notion
of sociology as the 'basic discipline of the social sciences', in some
sense the master-science of political practice, and liberal ideas of
equality and universal reason.

Mill was never able to resolve the conflict between his admiration of the ways in which Saint-Simon and Comte used theories of
history and his commitment to a structure of moral sciences founded
on a universal science of individual psychology. Mannheim's comparable difficulties motivate much more than he says in the discussions of *principia media*. Mannheim uses a sequence of historical

stages to present his case for planning, and he treats his central problem as a function of a distinctive historical constellation. Moreover, he acknowledges the parallels between the uses of *principia media* in his analysis and conceptions of historicist writers. But he strongly disassociates himself from them. 'Superficial insight into [the] character [of *principia media*]', he writes, 'has led many thinkers to speak of a special historical logic and has misled them into believing that the individual destiny of each historical epoch is entirely independent of the general laws of events'.[14] Dialectical thinkers are not as arbitrary as Romantic ones, he maintains, but they are 'also inclined to use unscientific methods. In its concrete form, [the dialectic] is mainly inspired by a philosophy of history, which draws its vision of the course of history from the particular aims of certain groups.'[15]

But Mannheim had not thought through very clearly just what he was upholding with his defence of universal factors against historicist challenges. He wanted to revise his earlier conceptions of alternative modes of sociological knowledge, but he had not worked out how he would interrelate the distinct types. What *is* clear is the undertaking to read situations as structures of alternative historical possibilities, while retaining the legitimacy of these readings and the controls upon them, which, he thought, only the systematized scientific disciplines could provide. Equally clear is Mannheim's growing mastery of the sociological literature and his interest in having results and ideas from the professional literature, for his use, while avoiding philosophically grounded complications. This attitude has less in common with Mill than it has with his predecessors in the Scottish School of Common Sense.[16]

And quite in the tradition of that school, it is Mannheim's concern with achieving changes in the way people relate to the world of public events and in the way in which they act which ultimately gives direction and coherence to Mannheim's multiple readings of the situation of his time. Underlying his reassessment of Enlightenment is a new emphasis on the demoralizing and brutalizing effects of disorientation and a corollary conception of the ethical regeneration to be achieved by building up a sense that knowledge of the way things are and where they are tending can be achieved and can be made practically effective. This requires more than the transmission of information; it requires the cultivation of a state of mind in which knowledge is experienced as needed and possible and in which there is confidence in the critical capacity to choose among conflicting accounts, to communicate with others having similar capacities, and to constitute sustained collaborations with them. The rhetorical tasks of forming his own audience and giving its members incentives and capacities to serve as audience, tasks having the highest dignity in the humanistic tradition he hoped to give modern life, strongly condition Mannheim's presentation of the thesis about the stage of planning, if not the thesis itself.

In a sense, Mannheim is caught in the modern version of an ancient vicious circle. If the need for planning arises out of the breakdown of the personality type capable of substantive rationality – i.e. responsible judgement grounded on balanced reading of the situation – the case for planning seems to require an audience of just this type. Only the enlightened, it seems, can be enlightened. Moreover, the personality required must also have some sort of public identity, responsibility, and role, since planning pertains to social relationships and institutions and not simply to the conduct of personal life. The ways of escaping from the circle which the theorists have developed may involve some conception of recalling the member of the audience to a deeper level of his 'nature', an expectation that the progress of 'history' is bringing the appropriate personality structure into being, or simply an analytical move radically distinguishing the logic of enquiry into the rational order of things from the logic of enquiry into practical choice. But Mannheim had challenged the simpler forms of such theories all of his life. Theories of 'dialectical' transformation of 'consciousness' come at the matter in ways which attempt to take into account the considerations which render simple theories of natural order, historical progress, or logical pluralism implausible. Much of Mannheim's work in Germany is informed by experimentation with such theories. Now this strategy too has come under pressure by events, as Mannheim understands them. He does not claim to have solved the dilemma about the interdependence between knowledge and moral development, which had already so deeply inspired the troubled Mill. Mannheim undertakes to manage the problem by appealing to the urgency of the crisis.

THREE DIMENSIONS OF CRISIS

Adapted long ago from the language of astrology and medicine, the concept of 'crisis' had come to play an influential part in the extensive social-diagnostic literature of the late nineteenth and early twentieth centuries. Mannheim's recourse to the *topos* derives from Marxist usage. Seen from this historical perspective, what are ordinarily called 'economic' crises, and particularly the culminating 'universal' crisis spell the doom of the social system afflicted by them, but by no means the death of the social organism. The accumulation of crises disrupts established patterns and uses of power, disturbing institutionalized order. Crises help to engender revolutionary class consciousness, and the final, decisive, universal crisis provides the occasion for the Great Revolution which will, once and for all, purge social life of the affliction attended by crises. Crisis, as it mounts, renders the old constraining grammar of action inoperative and irrelevant. But it opens the way to the creative ordering activity of revolution. What appears as confusion from the standpoint of the crisis proves to have another side. The disturbances which appear as symptoms of the crisis prove to be instrumental in the recovery – as the high fever during the crisis of a disease was thought to 'burn out' the disorder. In this Marxist usage, then, crises are understood as harbingers of a new order, radically different from the crisis-ridden one, but they gain this character only when understanding is taken as a call to action by forces which are, at one and the same time, products of the process and freed from it.

Crisis in this sense effectively obviates questions about political choices or 'value judgement'. The decision of what to work for or what to hope for is implicit in the acceptance of the diagnosis, although there is doubtless room for disagreement about the best way of overcoming the crisis. Whether reference is to the progress of an illness, a political venture, an economic process, or the transformation of society, crisis leaves no alternative to immediate, complete, and unambiguous response.

A diagnosis of crisis is a recurrent feature of Mannheim's cultural and sociological writings, and elements taken from the Marxist conception, duly transformed to strip them of their economic and political emphases, occur in his earliest work. But the concept first becomes a weighty factor in the claim that political ideology is in crisis, which grounds the argument in *Ideologie und Utopie*. Mannheim argues that the spread among all groups and parties of the insight into the social particularism of all social knowledge, its character as 'ideology', and the disorienting effect of that insight upon all groups and parties, as their doctrines are exposed and self-doubt is added to mistrust of all the others, create a crisis of practical political knowledge which breeds violence and passivity in place of political action. But when the knowledge initiated by insight into ideology is taken up by increasingly self-conscious intellectuals, it turns into the sociology of knowledge and develops into the science of politics. The sobering effects of the crisis-process itself prepare the groups and parties to renew the dialectical course of the political contest at a higher level, informed by the reading of the situation provided by the new science. In *Ideologie und Utopie*, Mannheim takes over a term from military language to epitomize the key linkage between his concepts of 'situation' and 'crisis'. He says that the ultimate objective of the sociology of knowledge as organon for a science of politics is to provide a 'situation-report' on the crisis.[17]

To see the crisis as 'situation' is to specify its place within the historical development and to recognize its constructive powers. Just a month before Hitler came to power, Mannheim published a short newspaper article on 'The Spiritual Crisis in the Light of Sociology'.[18] In it, he rejects the 'incorrect attitude' of those who interpret the crisis as a purely mental phenomenon and find in it nothing but the 'destruction of values'. Crises in personal and social life 'should not be placed under a magic ban or suppressed', he writes. The vital forces which they generate must be grasped. In order to do this, it is first necessary to appreciate that crises are not simply a product of the thoughts of people but of disorienting changes in their circumstances. Mannheim reports that he has even investigated this question by means of questionnaires and that he has found that only those who report such changes also claim to be in crisis. The course of vital spiritual processes, he maintains, is decisively influenced by 'our attitude . . . towards them, towards the crisis in our immediate environment and in our society as a whole'. It is the wrong attitude that brings about the 'deformations' and 'convulsions' which threaten to become habitual and irremediable. Where a false, overly intellectualistic attitude sees only 'decline', Mannheim concludes, it may well be that 'the new human being' is painfully emerging, by means of innumerable 'small, exhausting struggles'.[19]

But the most striking feature of the work after the Nazi seizure of power is the reality and immediacy ascribed to the possibility of 'chaos', and this changes the meaning of 'crisis'. In the opening pages of the published paper drawn from his 1933 talks in Holland, 'The Crisis of Culture in the Age of Mass-Democracies and Autarchies', Mannheim speaks repeatedly of the prospect of 'cultural disintegration', 'destruction', and even of 'cultural decline' in the sense made notorious by Oswald Spengler.[20] His later papers do not have quite that intensity of concern, but they also raise the possibility, quite unknown in the earlier writings, that the crisis will fuel regressive forces destructive of human civilization and culture. The 'next step' made possible by the situation may involve oppressive and dehumanizing forms of totalitarianism. The 'crisis' appears less as a crisis of transformation than as a crisis of survival.

This shift, by no means complete, brings Mannheim closer to the ways in which more conservative social thinkers have used the term. Mannheim himself once flatly asserted that 'the reaction usually plays on fears of chaos' in their social strategy.[21] The crisis is then described as disruption and threat and the diagnosis of crisis is generally conceived as a warning addressed to authority and as a call to restore order. The disease metaphor appears in conjunction with the identification of someone or something as the source of infection, which must be surgically removed or otherwise counteracted. When Mannheim warns the 'elite' against the rise of the 'masses', and proposes ways of strengthening the former and neutralizing the latter, he comes close to familiar authoritarian themes. His argument is almost never merely of this kind: the 'progressive' and 'conservative' connotations of 'crisis' are, rather, intermingled, and there are 'experimental' projections of alternative models. But the insistence on 'crisis' as a pervasive feature of the times is all-embracing.

In the collected essays in *Man and Society in an Age of Reconstruction*, Mannheim refers the crisis to three different dimensions, suggesting that distinct *principia media* are identified in each of these diagnoses and that the structured conjuncture of all three actually defines the situation, notwithstanding the fact that some of the trends counteract one another.

There is first the crisis of personality manifested in the loss of substantive rationality. This is the dimension where mass irrationality must first be countered by external manipulation based on behaviourist social psychology, and where qualitative changes leading to a restoration of responsibility in the full sense must be reserved for the comparatively few who can be helped by such therapies as socio-analysis and who can secure the recognition and carry on the activities without which such gains in consciousness are quickly lost. Eventually, it is hoped, planning of the first sort can be superseded by the second.

The special difficulty in this crisis arises from the fact that the instrumental rationalization, organizational as well as technical, undermining substantive rationality and responsibility, also creates instruments of mental control, especially in mass communications, which can be effectively wielded by irrational and irresponsible people. Those who might plan for the reconstitution of responsible personality are confronted by powerful opponents, who are also called to their mission, so to speak, by the crisis. The planners, although they aspire to more elevating means, must struggle with these opponents for mastery of the baser, manipulative means, and they must use those means to struggle for control over the masses.

Mannheim is quite aware of the paradox involved in this design. In the letter in which Mannheim responds gratefully to Oscar Jászi's reserved but fair review of *Mensch und Gesellschaft*, he avows himself a liberal in values like Jászi, insists that he is desperately attempting to utilize the instrumentalities controlling the modern world in order to salvage as many of those values as possible, and predicts that he will nevertheless soon join Jászi in Stoic despair.[22]

Mannheim concludes his most extensive discussion of this first dimension of the crisis with the question, 'Who plans the planner?'. His treatment of this question reveals a good deal about his adaptation of the 'crisis'-model in this context. Perhaps because the question may have arisen in the Christian circle in which he moved in the later years of his life, he professes to find it a 'religious' one, an expression of the fatalistic thought that our powers over all these things are finite, and events ultimately depend on forces which 'are beyond our reach and dominate us'. Without comment, he turns to the 'realistic and political sense' of the question, 'that no one has planned the planners' and that, accordingly, 'the planners can recruit themselves only from already existing groups'. 'Everything will . . . depend', he continues, 'on which of these groups with their existing outlooks will produce the energy, the decisiveness, and the capacity to master the vast social machinery of modern life.' His subsequent characterization of the groups is surprisingly almost wholly without social reference:

> Is it to be those groups in which traces of primitiveness . . .
> operate without restraint or those which have, through
> gradual education, developed their rational and moral
> capacities so far that they can act not only for a limited
> group, but also for the whole of society and bear the
> responsibility for it?

Although only 'small minorities' today possess the latter qualities, 'the masses always take the form which the creative minorities controlling societies choose to give them'.[23] Unlike his theory of the crisis of ideology, which accounts for the emergence of the intelligentsia called to overcome the critical impasse, Mannheim's theory of the crisis of substantive rationality does not offer a theoretical explanation of this 'creative minority'. Mannheim concludes with an 'open question' and an appeal to the reader to 'decide for himself'. The crisis of reason is met by an appeal to reason.

While the conception of personality which informs the diagnosis of crisis in the first of the three overlapping and partially conflicting readings of the situation is expressly liberal in antecedents, the central theme of the second one is the crisis attending the obsolescence of liberal social institutions. But here the analysis is much closer to a 'progressive' conception of crisis. The forces irremediably disrupting the liberal order have the inner capacity for constituting a new, higher level of order, and the crisis itself appears to create the conditions for bringing that reversal about.

According to Mannheim, the distinguishing feature of liberal society is the predominance of 'automatic' mechanisms for social integration. The equilibrium which is constantly reestablished by competition in the economic market is paradigmatic for comparable processes in other social domains, such as the balance of powers in internal and international relations, division of labour as a mode of uncoerced cooperation, a stabilizing balance between status and achievement as criteria for social advancement, and increasing satisfaction of social wants as a function of steadily rising social productivity. The cumulative effects of the operation of these mechanisms, however, create concentrations of power and means for participating in the processes which render the mechanisms ineffective or destructive. Viewed in another way, these novel key positions appear as elements in a new social order integrated by planning, although they are as yet either uncoordinated or blindly misdirected. There is already too much planning for the liberal order and not yet enough for the planned society, except where, as in England, some local situation has retarded or, as in Germany, forced the pace of development in symptomatic but inherently unsustainable way. The capability and the function are already real; their reality puts the social order in crisis; once this reality is recognized and consciously acted upon, the crisis will be transcended and the new order established.

This conception of a crisis of transition, since it does not envision revolutionary conflict and assigns decisive importance to the rise and spread of adequate scientific understanding alone, has more in common with Comtean Positivism than with Marxism. It also tends to neglect the fears about mounting irrationality and the disqualification for judgement which preoccupy Mannheim's reflections on the crisis in personality. From this standpoint, the emergence of totalitarian societies also loses some of its general significance. Instead of serving as a dreadful warning, it appears as a series of localized happenings, national societies driven into crude planning experiments by special circumstances.

Mannheim's third characterization of the crisis, in contrast, is his most pessimistic one. The crisis in culture threatens the life of the spirit, upon which Mannheim had grounded his dialectical readings of crisis during the Weimar years. He had already warned, in 1932, that 'democracy of intelligence' may turn into a 'democracy of the few' to 'mass democracy'. Mass democratization destroys the social conditions requisite to the work of intellectual elites and thus jeopardizes the ability to generate or to grasp the knowledge and the sensibility needed for cultural renovation. Even though the actual coordination of the diverse wills of social actors is carried on by political and organizational elites, social and political understanding ultimately depend, according to Mannheim, on the public interpretations created by intellectuals. A crisis in culture therefore ramifies beyond the cultural sphere in any narrow sense. Mannheim distinguishes four processes of 'negative democracy' or 'negative liberalism' rooted in the cultural sphere. He maintains that the sheer multiplication of 'elites', in numbers and types, cumulatively weakens the leadership function of the elite. Instead of some leading voices in each of the limited number of subsystems pertinent to any given individual in the compartmentalized liberal society, the individual receives diffuse and unmanageably varied signals and indications from many sources. Second, elites are deprived of the distance and exclusiveness needed to give them sufficient time and space to work out fully developed conceptions. The tempo of demands and opportunities characteristic of liberal society undergoing negative democratization means the distinctive styles or authoritative models cannot be created. There are only passing fashions.

Thirdly, according to Mannheim, the process of social selection has moved through a phase in which the democratic principle of achievement almost completely displaced the older principles of aristocratic breeding and wealth, a change which was itself unsettling though invigorating, into a phase marked by radically egalitarian principles, like the racial principle, which is a parody of the old aristocratic principle of blood. This threatens to destroy the very possibility of culture. Such an unwarranted extension of the struggle against privilege comes about when democratization

reaches the hitherto passive lower-middle classes. The enfranchise-
ment of the working class, in the broad sense, had not had these
consequences. The difference is that the lower-middle class cannot
accept or comprehend the rational development of modern society
and bitterly resents the hard truths brought out by cultural elites in
contact with the actual historical situation.

The make-up of the elite is also transformed by the expulsion of
the 'mobile' and cosmopolitan elements, which have provided the
dynamic force behind the distinctively modern cultural development
since the scholastic renaissance of the middle ages. Autochthonous
elements have served as valuable counter-balance within the cultural elites, but giving them monopoly control is socially regressive,
allied to autarchic tendencies in other social spheres, and hostile to
culture. Finally, Mannheim contends that the work of cultural elites
requires cultivated and stable publics as intermediaries between
cultural creators and the general population. He finds, however,
that such 'organic' publics are dissolved in the fluidity of mass society and that cultural creators become dependent on their ability to
drum together temporary audiences out of this mass. This can only
be done by creating sensations, he contends, or by otherwise appealing to a low common denominator. Mannheim brings this point
around to the crucial political domain, to account for the breakdown
of the political competition upon which his earlier comparatively
hopeful prognosis for the crisis of ideology had depended: In the
political sphere

> there was at the stage of the democracy of the few an
> intermediate body between the broad masses and the
> elites, as represented, for example, by the more or less
> constant electoral following and the different parties
> defined by the press. In the stage where democracy
> broadens into mass democracy, the role of those who have
> hitherto been non-voters, and of the younger generation
> which has not as yet made up its mind, becomes much
> more decisive as a fulcrum in (the) more or less definite,
> political, intermediate groups. . . . The parties which in
> liberal mass democracy strive to attain some importance,
> turn, for these very reasons, towards these as yet unorgan-
> ized masses and seek by appealing to emotional, irrational
> symbols, as these are understood by social psychology, to
> influence them in the desired direction.[24]

Mannheim insists that his reading of the situation is not antidemocratic in intention or consequences. The way out of the crisis must not be at the expense of the masses, by the establishment of some irresponsible power. He desiderates some forms of 'organization' that will achieve in a planned way what earlier 'organic' phases of culture had achieved by tradition or spontaneous social process. He cites two anticipations of such a development, oddly juxtaposed: the shift towards organized audiences associated with such schemes as trade-union sponsored workers' theatre; and the strict organization of its following instituted by the totalitarian parties after their attraction of voluntary adherents brought them to power. The theory of the crisis itself gives little reason to expect that to happen.

All three diagnoses of crises converge on the need for 'planning', i.e. strategic intervention in the situation based on a grasp of its structured interconnections. The trend towards planning noted in analysing the crisis of the liberal social order must overcome the trends towards catastrophic irrationality and the dissolution of culture. In one sense, Mannheim is convinced that it is bound to do so: integrative planning will come. But the 'planning' may take a form which merely suspends for a time the worst effects of the other two trends, while furthering underlying forces. Totalitarian 'planning' has this character, according to Mannheim. The question is how genuinely therapeutic planning can come about.

In the liberal age, the wholly spontaneous integrative social mechanisms had been supplemented by the coordinative effects of parliamentary politics and law. And in his essay on politics as a science, Mannheim had proposed an alternative conception of politics, as the practical domain in which novelties are created to deal with situations not amenable to the rational analyses of liberalism or to the predictabilities of administration. Now Mannheim does not envision that either of these conceptions can explain how the crisis might give way to planning.

Planning is itself much like politics in that it also deals with 'situations'. But now Mannheim does not welcome the similarity as infusing vital and creative dynamism in society. He cheerfully sees planning itself as transitional to universal administration, which

> emerges as soon as the social structure passes from the stage of planning into a completely organized state, and as soon as all or most of the historical forces, which have arisen in the struggle, have been brought under control through strategy.[25]

History itself appears as the enemy:

It is also possible that at a later stage all that we now call history, namely the unforeseeable, fateful dominance of uncontrolled social forces, will come to an end. As contrasted with administration, planning is thus a form of conduct still operating within the framework of history. As we understand it, planning is foresight deliberately applied to human affairs, so that the social process is no longer merely the product of conflict and competition.[26]

Mannheim's ideal now appears as the universal pacification which he had once derided as an illusion of liberalism and which he had projected as marking the end of all human striving, and thus of all human knowledge as well. It appears as an anti-utopian utopia.

In a brief speculation, responding to the challenge from the rightist sociologist, Hans Freyer, that there must be a political 'will to planning' somewhere, if the intellectual design is to have any effect, Mannheim finds an interesting and revealing historical precedent of an end to conflictual politics in the early modern period in Europe. Is it not possible he wonders, that 'there should now emerge, following this great tide of irrationalism, a new readiness to listen to reason', as happened 'after the Wars of Religion' in the sixteenth century 'when religious fanaticism and irrationality in general were in a certain sense transcended'. He concedes that only small elites achieved statesmanlike insights and Machiavellian *Realpolitik* in the earlier instance, but he asks whether the masses now moving toward disillusionment, when their present experiences of communal ecstasy prove false, may not as a result collectively receive such political education. 'It should not be forgotten,' he adds, 'that the labor movement, which is typically rational in its attitude towards the social process, began as a machine-wrecking movement.'[27]

But this echo of Marxist analysis, implausibly associated with a concept of 'masses' expressly designed as an alternative to Marxist expectations about classes as coherent social actors, is little more than a wish. In any case, there is nothing in the argument to suggest that the 'masses' can themselves initiate political action. At best, they may prove able to 'listen to reason', as laid out for them by post-political planners. Mannheim is adamant against the Marxist model of social transformation through class conflict. He denies that classes are the sole or even primary social actors under condition of mass society, and he rejects the thought that conflict can overcome the crisis. Competition and conflict now imply chaos.

In *Ideologie und Utopie*, Mannheim's conception of politics had been much less obsessed by the fear of social disintegration. Without faith in Marxist visions of revolution, he nevertheless emphasizes the value of class conflict. He calls for 'a new knowledge' and a new 'synthesis' but he sees this as rising out of the *Realdialektik* of political contestation, when spiritualized by the insights of intellectuals. He denies that 'progressive' political and social development involves, as Romantic critics of liberal progressivism had contended, a mechanical rationalization of the world, abstracted from the deeper authenticities of pre-rational human experience and hostile to emotion, unpredictability, novelty, and creativity.

Mannheim's diagnoses of the threefold crises of mass society, as they appear to him in exile, largely vitiate such a solution of his initial and central problems. Spirit, social knowledge, and politics do not work – or do not work any longer – as this conception expects. Theory and practice are not integrated as the essay on politics as a science had thought. Mannheim had always hedged his commitment to this approach and cultivated alternative conceptions more modest in their speculative sweep and more narrowly oriented to the academic discipline of sociology. Now he was trying to use the elements of this alternative approach to build an intellectual strategy for comprehending a thesis at least as sweeping in scope as that which his earlier recourse to philosophy of history had meant to embrace.

Planning is itself a concept meant to interrelate theory and practice, an alternative to merely technological conceptions of applied science. As a comprehensive understanding of 'situations', this thinking has an inherent practical capacity, in Mannheim's view, with the knowledge of *principia media* approximating to the science of the political art of which Mill and Comte had spoken. But the theory of planning as a way of thinking does not explain how theory can turn into practice, how planning can become a way of governing. It is too paradoxical to count on 'enlightenment' in any simple sense, when the theoretical explanation for the necessity of change depends so heavily on the experience of a mounting irrationality. Mannheim works with the analogy of psychotherapy to account for a knowledge with inherent and immediate transformative effect and he repeatedly invokes the parallel of Socratic questioning, the great paradigm of another sort of therapy for another sort of soul. But all of these approaches still leave unanswered the questions of who plans the planners, who legitimates and installs them as planners. The diagnosis of crisis is not so much meant to answer these questions as it is to avoid their being pressed.

Mannheim puts his case quite clearly, in an essay written just before the war:

> It has often been said that planning is possible in the democratic countries only in the case of war. In a time of crisis, with victory as the goal, it would be easy to obtain public recognition of a single purpose and an ultimate value. The question is: Can a planned society, especially in the present period of transition, work out a number of vital purposes that are clearly determined by necessity, without the need for war? Thereby, a problem, which may be quite insoluble on the theoretical plane, where all values – at least at the present moment – seem to be relative, can be instantly solved in practice. The philosophical dilemma is considerably simplified by the fact that our whole society finds itself in an almost military state of emergency.[28]

Mannheim speaks of the 'plane' as 'theoretical' and the 'dilemma' as 'philosophical', like the theoretical inconsistencies between the premises underlying behavioural and psychoanalytical approaches, which he similarly sought to bypass by a pragmatic injunction to get on with the practical work. But the cases are quite dissimilar. Here the question is inescapably a political one as well, since the 'relativism' of values refers to conflicts among social actors demanding different things, and not merely to problems of philosophical foundations of values.

The formulation makes it clear that Mannheim is well aware that such agreement on common purposes does not in fact exist. The diagnosis of crisis must itself rhetorically forge the unity presupposed by the thesis of the 'planned society'. The crisis takes the place of 'revolution' in the Marxist approach, objectively and subjectively. In its supposed historical reality, it breaks the social resistance to change, and in its being recognized, it constitutes the actors to bring the change about. The planners, in short, are those cognizant of the crisis. The agreement on crisis implies agreement on what is 'necessary'; it implies agreement that the emergency is too great for the luxury of disagreement. Crisis sets the priorities for enquiry and the standards for action. It mobilizes the key actors and legitimizes their counsel. If the creation of a synthesis to orient the politics envisioned in *Ideologie und Utopie* required the intellectuals to serve as prophetic watchmen, the realization of planning appears to depend on a self-fulfilling prophecy.

PROBLEMS OF HISTORY

In the earlier work, Mannheim's model was closer to Lukács's version of Marxism: the crisis furthers the actualization of consciousness, through dialogue among the principal social voices. Action informed by such heightened consciousness will be adequate to the situation. The catalytic function performed by the sociology of knowledge cultivated by the intellectuals is to bring out of the mutual recriminations about the ideological character of the opponents' social thinking the understanding of social structure which Mannheim believed to be implicit there. Awareness of ideology is already potentially synthetic social knowledge. The initial move proposed is a reflective one: social thinkers are invited to become aware of what they are about. This reflection, then, will open the structure of social life to reflective thinkers through a recontextualizing of their own ideologies, since they will become aware that their identities are socially constituted. They will, in short, be led by the crisis to see through the crisis to the dialectical historical development underneath, in which they will recognize their own situation and their own roles. Thus understood, crisis is a moment in history; it is not an end to history.

In the subsequent work, written out of a deep sense of chronological and cultural discontinuity, the diagnosis of crisis assumes a much heavier burden. Nicolaus Sombart characterizes the concept of crisis developed by Saint-Simon and Comte as follows:

> The concept of crisis, as employed first by Saint-Simon and then by Comte, is completely novel in intellectual history. It has remained the central concept of the modern understanding of the times. It refers to the Revolution; but since it sees through the political surface of events, it opens social–historical reality to view, in its totality. In other words, when Saint-Simon speaks of crisis, he is the first to refer to history in an altogether modern sense. But if revolution and history are both crisis, does this not amount to putting an end to revolution, and end to history? And it is indeed the case that the end of revolution will be the end of history – at least, of history as we know it. And what comes after? . . . Rule by sociologists.[29]

As Mannheim moved further from historicism, his conception of the crisis directed itself ever more thoroughly against historical subjectivity. His seminal essay on the concept of 'thought at the level of planning', '*principia media*', and the 'problem of transforming man' opens with the proposition that man has 'taken a new step forward when he can live his own history in the spirit of experiment and create out of the emergent forces of the social process the knowledge and will to shape history itself'. This new relationship between human actors and the events of their past and present experience is expounded first by means of a contrast with the view of history exemplified in 'the older epic form of historiography' which 'placed the individual man and individual events in the foreground'. The 'sociological view', in contrast, 'sees history as a field of experiment and reform'. Corresponding to this, according to Mannheim, is a new mode of 'self-observation' documented in autobiographies. Mannheim contends that 'the modern observer . . . is concerned with himself mainly in so far as he can use his knowledge of the origins of his psychological defects as a universal remedy for society as a whole'. 'This form of self-analysis,' he maintains, 'has a levelling tendency and disregards individual differences because it is concerned with the general aspects of the human personality and its capacity for transformation'. It is remarkable, in the light of Sombart's comments, that Mannheim finally takes as paradigm case of the new view of conducting one's life the 'experimental' life of Saint-Simon, as characterized by Lorenz von Stein.[30]

In his introduction to the English version of *Man and Society in an Age of Reconstruction*, Mannheim drives home the point of the contrast between 'epic' and 'sociological' readings of self and history. He distinguishes between the 'function' of his book in its original German and revised English versions: in the former case, it was 'an attempt at self-enlightenment made for the benefit of those who have actually lived through these experiences' and who consequently 'experience' 'the collapse of liberalism and democracy and the adoption of a totalitarian system' as a 'transition' which is 'a change in the very structure of modern society'. Now the book must communicate with a readership 'which has only hearsay knowledge of such changes and is wrapped in an illusion of traditional stability'. They are inclined to localize the crisis, to see it as part of the aftermath of the Great War and similar to the many instances in history when dictatorships have been established 'as temporary solutions in an emergency'. But they must be brought to appreciate that what is happening in the 'danger zone' or the 'crisis zone' is a 'phase of disintegration' which is only slower to show its symptoms in the 'countries which still enjoy comparative peace', so that they may take steps to avoid 'the negative aspects of the process' which 'were often only bewildered attempts to deal with the concrete difficulties in which these countries were suddenly involved'. Timing and intensity belong to history; the process inheres in the structure.[31] To grasp the process, it is necessary to move out of historical space and time, as those have been defined by immediate experience, and to live in the crisis, in the world of social structures in dissolution and reconstruction and in the objective temporality of phases, transitions, and ages.

Mannheim is aware of the perplexing nature of the interplay he is demanding between disembodied and yet anthropomorphized 'forces' and acting 'men'. He writes:

> Processes are at work . . . which can only find fulfilment (*sic*) in a new form of planning. As long as the social forces are left to themselves, conflict breaks out just when they (*sic*) are on the point of reaching a solution. But it is due to human inadequacy, and not merely to the social forces themselves, that men fail (*sic*) at the eleventh hour to build these latent tendencies into a workable system. At a certain stage of development it is not enough to leave external trends to themselves (*sic*); we need a new type of man who can see the right thing to do, and new political groups which will do it. . . . (Today) there are indications that if the groups engaged in politics still refuse to look beyond their own immediate interests, society will be doomed. At the present stage of events we need a new kind of foresight, a new technique for managing conflicts, together with a psychology, morality, and plan of action in many ways completely different from those which have obtained in the past. It is only by remaking man himself that the reconstruction of society is possible.[32]

Since Mannheim also argues that 'remaking man' requires the insight and actions of a 'new type of man', the problem appears insoluble.

As so often before, Mannheim turns to sincere and disarming personal statement. 'The writer feels it is better to confess,' he writes, 'that he is only groping his way.'

> A time will probably come when it will be easy to describe the events in our own lives or in the life of the community, not in narrative form, but in a series of sociological problems and conflicts. To try to translate them into these terms today is like exploring a new country. . . . This

incompleteness. . . has influenced the form of this book. It
is a series of essays. . . . (H)ere and there contradictory
statements have not been reconciled where they seem to
express the genuine predicament of our thought. . . . (If)
there is to be a science of politics and of society there must
be no obligation to find a definite solution before the time
is ripe.[33]

This apology is linked to an extended justification for the
speculative character of his enquiry, which Mannheim clearly
expects to be criticized by the learned community. He claims that
the projection of theoretical models is essential in the social sciences
and challenges the stress on measurement and the accumulation of
facts. 'The established sciences unconsciously try to belittle the newcomer,' he observes. 'Every branch of science is expert . . . at creating inhibitions and defence mechanisms which bar the way to a
complete and adequate knowledge of society.'[34]

The discontinuities which enter into the structure of Mannheim's work as refugee are not limited to those engendered by the
shocking and seemingly abrupt turn of things in German political
life, rendering the historical calculation of contesting forces and the
projection of a 'next step' irrelevant. Nor are they only a question of
the disorienting break in cultural life, as the shared cultivation and
spiritual community proved to be ephemeral and fellow-intellectuals
and academic colleagues fell enthusiastically into the marching
ranks. Mannheim also suffered profoundly under the requirement of
making his thoughts understood in an alien language to people he
considered to be largely closed to the mode of knowledge he had to
offer. In time, he came to pride himself on his success as mediator
between cultural traditions and on his acceptance in the community
of English scholars and gentlemen, but his method was profoundly
affected by the effort at adjustment. Parallel to his attempt, by way
of the appeal to crisis, to break through all the historical particular-
isms of speaker and audience to a shared condition of being in effect
a social function within a given state of the social system, Mannheim
also attempted to gain recognition from the English audience and to
establish living contact with them, in a shared historical setting. His
works are conditioned by these two contradictory responses to this
central problem.

TWO CULTURES: TRANSLATION PROBLEMS

Mannheim's sensitivity to inner connections between cultural variations and the modes of theoretical discourse appropriate to social
theory is already evident in 1917 in his review of a work by Ernst
Cassirer. Despite scepticism about some of Cassirer's claims, Mannheim agrees that the link between 'national character' and 'intellectual mission' will manifest itself more precisely in the forms than
in the contents of intellectual productions. 'We come closer to the
solution [of this problem] through style analyses in art and literary
history and by examining the distinctive dialectics, the capacity for
systems construction, and the incidence of thought patterns in cognitive acts,' he writes.[35] Questions about varieties of knowing and
about the ways in which new knowledge depends upon authentic
grounding in contexts of existing knowledge, upon co-participation
in social projects of knowing, are the stuff of much of his subsequent
work. Sometimes those contexts are conceived as 'systematizations',
related to, though not identical with, disciplinary frames of reference, and sometimes they appear as various types of socio-historical
entities – experiential communities, social classes, generations,
groups bound to a location in the social and historical process. In his
ambitious methodological treatise of the mid-1920s, Mannheim had
distinguished between the kind of abstract and technical knowledge
which can be universally communicated, translated from language
to language and place to place, and the interpretive identity-defining
and action-constituting knowledge which is rooted in some sort of
mutual connectedness and contagion. Within that model itself, there
is provision for intercommunal synthesis, mediated by special strata,
open to diverse currents and able to create interactions; and Mannheim's subsequent move towards sociology of knowledge corrects
the tendency to restrict authentic meanings to 'communities', in the
sense in which conservatives had contrasted that term to 'societies'.
But there is never any doubt that social knowledge has a deep
rhetorical dimension, depending for its validity on the resonances
and association it generates in those to whom it pertains. And Mannheim's own position in his German work is always carefully
developed with sympathetic reference to the present state of the
intellectual domain, presenting itself as a reflection upon what is
going on, a 'following after' and experimental extrapolation.

After his appointment at Frankfurt in 1930, Mannheim expres-
sed his interest in American social research, and he took pride in
differing from his more traditional colleagues in this respect. At the

same time, he always insisted on the situational specificity of that research, which he regarded as untheoretical in character, and he reserved the right to recontextualize its findings within interpretive frameworks emerging out of his own theorizing. When he sent *Ideologie und Utopie* to the American sociologist, Louis Wirth, who had requested the book during a short visit to Mannheim and who was eventually responsible for its English translation, Mannheim writes:

> Since I have experienced in my own case and in that of others how difficult it is for a mere examination to do full justice to an investigation which emerges in a different setting, I would ask you, in the spirit of our conversation, not to take a final position on our sociological efforts until you have a chance of living with us for a while and of seeing how we pose scientific problems from within the immediate problem context of our life here.[36]

For a short time and on rare occasions after his arrival in Germany in 1919, Mannheim had spoken of himself as an Hungarian exile, using his observations of Germany to clarify his own sense of national identity, but this was never more than one of his brief experiments, altogether replaced – as far as his public and literary personae are concerned – by complete identification with German cultural life. In England, however, he presented himself as the refugee, the outsider seeking a haven and bringing in return the wisdom earned by his sufferings. This mode mixed oddly with the presentation of himself as the sociologist who is by profession the master of a knowledge reaching beyond the surface variety of historical events. Yet it is the mixture of the two which shapes both manner and matter of his English work.

In Germany, he was satisfied that he could show that the kind of sociology he represented grew out of and entered into the spirit of intellectual and political life. His work on conservative thought had that as one of its major theses, and his vigorous defence of sociology of knowledge against the charge of 'sociologism', as enunciated, for example, by the influential German Romanist, Ernst Robert Curtius, was precisely its continuity with the philosophical tradition of the great German classics.[37] His contrasting initial reading of the English situation is captured in a letter written by Mannheim to Wirth, on July 26th, 1933, to announce his acceptance of a temporary position at the London School of Economics.[38]

Mannheim begins by explaining his reasons for not awaiting

the outcome of his discussions with representatives of the 'University in Exile', to be associated with the New School of Social Research in New York, before accepting the opportunity offered in London:

> What was morally and psychologically decisive for me was [Harold] Laski's statement that it would be my task, in collaboration with [Morris] Ginsberg and himself, finally and truly to establish sociology in England. It really is inconceivable that, in a time that can move forward only on the basis of sociological knowledge, a world power like England still rejects this study. You will understand that one would rather go where one has the feeling or the illusion of being needed, and that one is not called simply out of pity for one's troubles.

Nevertheless, he fears that Laski is overly optimistic. The chances for success are slight. 'England strikes me as too self-assured a nation,' he writes, 'and the intellectuals too little inwardly unsettled, to call into question the philosophical–historical–aesthetic academic routine and to recognize that life challenges us with new questions.'

The experiences of the next five years confirmed Mannheim's fears. His choice of problems and publications as well as the design of his work bear the marks of his attempts to overcome this difficulty. The same letter to Wirth reports, for example, that he is still hopeful that J. C. B. Mohr (Paul Siebeck), his German publisher, will bring out his book on 'the sociology of the spirit', which will include the essay on generations published earlier, and a long study of intellectuals. In the manuscript, which he claims to have completed, there may also have been a text upon which the posthumously published 'Towards the Sociology of the Mind' was based.[39] What is striking is that there is neither record not testimony to suggest that he ever made any effort to publish these works in English, or the two methodological essays of the early 1920s, published posthumously as *Structures of Thinking*, which he had kept with him in multiple copies and which he edited in the last year of his life.

Mannheim writes Wirth that while the United States might better enable him to continue his actual work, he feels obliged to stay in England for a while and to work with young people on the study of the German catastrophe. But whether he will be able to contribute to the discipline even in this way is very uncertain, he concludes, since the English atmosphere is thick with self-satisfaction and very few recognize that every effort is needed to preserve the cultured world from destruction.

Mannheim's judgement of the difficulties emerges especially well in his treatment of the sociology of knowledge, to which he is referring when he writes to Wirth about 'the work he was forced to abandon in Frankfurt'. At times, he seems to have put it altogether behind him. Just before the war he writes about the need to learn 'a new experimental attitude in social affairs', in view of the 'practical deterioration of the ideals of Liberalism, Communism, and Fascism'. He continues:

> But one can only learn if one has belief in the power of reason. For a time it was healthy to see the limitations of *ratio*, especially in social affairs. It was healthy to realize that thinking is not powerful if it is severed from the social context and ideas are only strong if they have their social backing, that it is useless to spread ideas which have no real function and are not woven into the social fabric. But this sociological interpretation of ideas may also lead to complete despair, discouraging the individual from thinking about issues which will definitely become the concern of the day. This discouragement of the intelligentsia may lead them to too quick a resignation of their proper function as the thinkers and forerunners of the new society, may become even more disastrous in a social setting where more depends on what the leading elites have in mind than in other periods of history.[40]

Mannheim goes on to argue that the theory of the social determination of ideas properly applied to the present age shows that everything depends on 'whether or not sound thinking goes on today and whether it reaches the ruling elites'. Elsewhere, of course, his criterion of 'healthiness' does yield a function for the sociology of knowledge: it is understood as having a therapeutic function in freeing the mind for 'sound thinking', insofar as it may still be clouded by misleading, ideological notions dictated by group egoisms.

But these shifts in his thinking about the usefulness of the sociology of knowledge, are balanced by several counter-considerations. In the first place, even in England his standing as a sociologist and thus his legitimacy as diagnostician of the crisis were founded, above all, on the wide recognition given *Ideologie und Utopie* and associated publications. When the Professor of Sociology at the London School of Economics, Morris Ginsberg, reviewed a number of basic textbooks and handbooks in sociology in February, 1933, before Mannheim's ouster from Frankfurt, he called attention to Mannheim's article on 'Wissenssoziologie' in Vierkandt's *Handwörterbuch der Soziologie*. Linking sociology of knowledge with Max Weber's 'work on the relation between religious systems and economic development', he expresses the hope that it would be 'helpful' in making less vague the general consideration that Robert MacIver and Leonard Hobhouse had given the relationship between 'the growth of mind and society', which Ginsberg regards as the central problem in evolutionary theory, his own major interest.[41] Ginsberg's expectations in this regard doubtless entered into the complex relationship between the two men in subsequent years. Mannheim's original sponsor at the London School of Economics, Harold Laski, had long been interested in the social interpretation of political ideas, although he inclined ever more towards a Marxist rendering of the nature and role of political theory. Speaking at a conference on the social sciences in 1935, which Mannheim and Ginsberg also addressed, Laski remarks:

> Theories . . . have an ancestry and its investigation alone gives us the clue to its understanding. More than that. It gives us a clue to the validity of ideas. For they emerge always as a statement of the thinker's idea of a good to be realised; and this is born of . . . the environment to which he belongs . . ., no more than a magisterial summary of certain tendencies of his time.[42]

Second, his primary link to American sociology, where he expected a better reception than in England, is Louis Wirth, professor in the prestigious Chicago department and since 1931 editor of the *American Journal of Sociology*. After Wirth's original visit to him in 1930, their correspondence had led to the agreement for Wirth to assist in the publication of an English translation of *Ideologie und Utopie* and to write 'an interpretive introduction that will introduce the average American reader to the problem area and show him the right way to get into it'. Wirth suggests inclusion of the *Handwörterbuch* article as well. Mannheim's insecure position in 1933 and his hope that Wirth could find him an American appointment made this project all the more important to him.

The English edition of *Ideology and Utopia*, which differs from the German *Ideologie und Utopie* in ways that cannot be attributed to normal translation difficulties, is the product of Mannheim's own adaptations of the translation prepared by Edward Shils, under the largely nomial supervision of Wirth. Since there has been some disagreement about this in the literature on Mannheim, it seems worth emphasizing that all the documentary evidence available, primarily the correspondence between Wirth and Mannheim, confirms the recollections of Shils and Jean Floud, who helped Mannheim in this work. And the direction of the departures from the original text coincides with the direction of Mannheim's development in his other English work.[43] It is not meaningful to ask whether these were changes in theoretical convictions or simply conceptual adjustments to obviate problems in communication, because the important rhetorical constituent in Mannheim's conception of theoretical adequacy, his concern with the effects of knowledge upon the ethical and political constitution of the audience, makes issues of conviction and communication interdependent. In any case, the adjustments are radically incomplete, and the book in English has fascinated several generations, while inviting the most varied and arbitrary interpretations by its many inconsistencies.

A dramatic contrast between the two versions concerns the starting point. The German work begins with the crisis of mutual distrust: all social actors denounce the statements of all the others as mere ideology, exposing their roots in the particular volitions of the groups concerned. It is the presumed experience of this crisis which forms the existential presupposition for the sociology of knowledge. The knowledge creating this crisis, the ways in which each social group adapts the originally Marxist insight to its own ideology, opens the groups to the synthesizing intervention of the intellectuals and their organon. Now none of this can any longer be presupposed.

Mannheim asks Wirth to open the way to the English-speaking reader. When Mannheim receives Wirth's historical appreciation and summary overview, cast in the idiom of American academic pragmatism, his praise is almost effusive:

> I have read [your introduction] twice, with great attentiveness and dedication, and I can say that it gave me great joy. That came not only from your profound understanding of the time and circumstances out of which the book arose, but also from your interpretation of the thoughts I sought to develop – the like of which I have never met with, despite the extensive literature on the subject.[44]

He puts particular emphasis on the communicative significance of Wirth's accomplishment:

> I never would have thought that persons from altogether
> different worlds, with differing scientific traditions could
> have approached one another so closely. The conscious-
> ness of this is much more important to me than any exter-
> nal success: it is a guarantee for spiritual cooperation
> among the intellectuals in the contemporary world.

Although he concludes these words of praise with the claim that he
is 'convinced that this introduction will bring the book across to the
Anglo-Saxon reader', he closes the letter with the surprising
announcement that he is at work on a new opening for the book
because he has 'not been satisfied with the opening . . . looked at
from the standpoint of the Anglo-Saxon reader'. When that rework-
ing turns into the manuscript subsequently published as 'A Preliminary Approach to the Problem', Wirth responds with irritation.
There would be too many introductions; there are new departures
that might 'obscure the burden of the book itself'; the work has
historical importance, in its original form.[45] But Mannheim
insists, because of 'the situation here in England':

> If the book were to appear only in America, I would . . .
> publish it in the old form. . . . The great security which
> rules in this nation has not opened the minds of even the
> most clear-headed among the local intellectuals to the
> problem of the sociological antecedents of consciousness.
> Most would consider the old book as nothing more than a
> document from a world closed to them.[46]

The primary difficulties, in short, derive from the English sense
of their own historical identity and from the historical time within
which they move, Mannheim implies, and he proposes to overcome
them 'by means of the historical analogies with the Sophists and
Socrates, by means of an historical sketch of this mode of thinking'.
Additional difficulties arise, he maintains, from the fact that there 'is
no tradition of sociology, one might say'. It is necessary to say
'something' about a 'conception of empiricism which can be something more than counting, measuring, or describing'. Otherwise,
every English reader would put the book aside as 'too abstract'.
Moreover, Mannheim contends, it is necessary for him to emphasize
even more clearly that these are only exploratory essays so that the
book is not subjected to the sorts of misjudgements which were
inflicted upon it by some German critics. Wirth made no further
protest and Shils proceeded to translate the German text.

Mannheim's activist conception of theoretical discourse is well brought out in the imagery he uses in further reconciling Wirth to the new situation:

[Your] preface and the new opening of the book together ensnare the reader into the problem context in concrete form, so that later, once interested in the matter, he allows some things to happen to him that do not correspond to his tradition.[47]

Mannheim's 'preliminary approach', in fact, suggests more about the philosophical background to the original essays than either Wirth's introduction or Mannheim's revised version of the translation, because the humanist and rhetorical tradition to which Mannheim relates his work, presumably in order to accommodate the old-fashioned education of the English, bears very strongly on its structure. But Mannheim is more interested in reorienting the direction of the work than he is in recapturing this aspect of its design.

While Mannheim rushed through the writing of the 'preliminary approach' and had not time to revise the translation, he spent several months on the main body of the text. The effect of the work is changed, first, by the transformation of the theoretical vocabulary, moving it from the universe of philosophical discourse of the post-Hegelian German *Geisteswissenschaften* towards the psychological frames of reference of English post-utilitarian philosophy of mind, with its characteristic emphasis on distinctions between judgements of facts and judgements of values, or American pragmatism. 'Spirit' (*Geist*) becomes 'mind' or 'intellect'; 'consciousness' (*Bewusstsein*) becomes 'mental activity' or 'evaluation'; the various terms for the objective directedness of the will, its tendency towards one or another state of things, become 'interests', 'purposes', 'norms', or 'values'; 'primaeval structures of mind' become 'irrational mechanisms'; and 'false consciousness' is divided between 'erroneous knowledge' and 'invalid ethical attitude'. Cumulatively, the distinctive claims about the inner connections among social location, practical design, and social knowledge characteristic of sociology of knowledge as organon become difficult to grasp.

In the German version, Mannheim says that the 'evaluative concept of ideology' '*makes* judgements concerning the reality of ideas and structures of consciousness'; according to the English version, it 'presupposes' such judgements.[48] More broadly, if 'evaluations' based on 'interests' introduce 'bias' into 'thinking', creating 'erroneous knowledge' and 'invalid ethical attitudes' lacking in 'objectivity', there seems little reason for giving the resultant 'ideologies' the measure of credence implied in all the talk about 'relationism'. The structure of social knowledge no longer appears as ontologically grounded, as knowledge in its social and historical nexus. Its constitutive stylistic principle is no longer conceived simply as an 'ontological decision', with all the difficulties about the interworking between rational and irrational elements that this implies; ideologies appear more nearly as analysable compounds of empirical 'ontology' and 'value judgement'.

A slight terminological emendation in the subtitle of the central essay signals the important shifts under way. The main title in German is in the form of a question, 'Is Politics as a Science Possible?' The English equivalent, 'The Prospects of Scientific Politics', loses the two allusions in the German title – to Weber's two essays, 'Politics as a Vocation' and 'Science as a Vocation', and to the Kantian question about the 'possibility' of one or another kind of knowledge, which plays such an important part in Mannheim's own epistemological and methodological reflections. Moreover, the change from 'politics as science' to 'scientific politics' reduces the multiple possibilities left open by the German terms to one. The German could mean that politics itself becomes a mode of 'scientific' enquiry, interrogating reality so as to achieve orientation and mastery; it could mean, quite to the contrary, that a political science comes into being which studies scientifically the partially irrational activity of politics; or it could mean what the English does. Mannheim's essayistic approach in German is designed to play these possibilities off against one another without settling on any one of them. His design in the English version is different.

The change in the subtitle leaves no doubt that it is not simply a matter of inevitable or unnoticed linguistic loss. The German subtitle simply refers to 'Theory and Practice', and it corresponds to the substantive issue with regard to which the illustrative sociology of knowledge exercise in the chapter is to serve as 'organon'. The English subtitle is 'The Relationship between Social Theory and Political Practice'. The two activities are analytically separated, as in *Man and Society*, and the way is opened to the possibility that 'scientific politics' will supersede 'political practice', in the sense worked out in the chapter. Of course, the chapter does not get to such supersession; it is, after all, a translation of the German essay. But its argument becomes less coherent, and the special role of the 'intellectuals', increasingly portrayed as possessing a governing knowledge, dramatically overshadows the recourse to the 'practical dialectics' of political life.

These conceptual modifications and other methodological changes amount to a substantial adjustment in the theoretical structure. In a footnote to the discussion of the 'school' which is the practical outcome of the enquiry into theory and practice, Mannheim extrapolates from his immediate argument. He calls the reader's attention to the fact that the main text has come upon the 'correct' answer to the question about the type of schooling needed, and that it has done so through nothing more than 'concrete analysis of situations', like that pursued by the sociology of knowledge. The goal of his entire investigation would be attained, Mannheim avers, if he were able to formulate the logic according to which the result was attained. He concludes: 'A genuine situational analysis of a style of thought would have to be able to specify the measure of its validity'. Mannheim eliminates the footnote from his English version.[49]

More generally, then, the sociology of knowledge is moved further away from being a mode in which Mannheim, as essayist, participates reflectively in the common spiritual life present in politics and towards being a science which its practitioners use in order to offer causal explanations for a certain class of political events. The author does not offer himself to the political reader as someone engaged in a shared project, engaged in self-clarification, and hoping that thinking the critical situation through will itself bring about a turning towards realistic practice. Although the contents remain rich in ambiguities, the form moves from the sophisticated, reflective essay towards the scientific treatise. And the latter form makes demands on the rigour, precision, and economy of the presentation, which the work cannot meet.

Mannheim was very bitter about the reception accorded *Ideology and Utopia* in the major professional journals of American sociology. The *American Sociological Review* published a review by Alexander von Schelting, who had been Mannheim's editor for the published excerpt from his *Habilitationsschrift* on conservatism and who had criticized *Ideologie und Utopie* when it first appeared in German. Mannheim rages in a letter to Wirth. He had earlier cited von Schelting's German critique as the sort of criticism he hoped to forestall by publishing the 'Preliminary Approach'. Now he complains that von Schelting has ignored his express statements that the book documents a search, that the essays reflect the fact that several systems may be operating at one time within an individual, and that 'experimental thinking' must express this variety, in order to test the systems. Mannheim asserts that he could easily 'make Schelting impossible'. His neo-Kantian philosophical objections have been undermined by discoveries about the genesis of 'meanings'. Mannheim claims that the whole affair is at so low a level, involving someone without standing or competence, that there must be a manoeuvre against him, 'or at least against the tendency which identifies with me'. There is no other reason to bring such a person forward, when there are so many better qualified reviewers among the young refugees. He asks Wirth whether he should answer, whether Wirth would give him space in the *American Journal of Sociology*, or whether it would be better to have some third person write the reply.[50] There is no record of Wirth's answer, but the review that appeared in the University of Chicago Journal gave Mannheim no solace. Once again, the book was given to a younger refugee scholar; and Hans Speier raised many of the same sorts of objections as von Schelting, charging philosophical confusion and a lack of sociological realism about the role of intellectuals. Mannheim is moved to gloomy thoughts, premature for a 44-year-old:

> It keeps happening these days . . . that the next generation is glad to be lifted into the saddle by us, live by our inspiration, and then, for careerist reasons, will know nothing more of it and deny a person at the next best opportunity. I can't help thinking of Speier and Schelting in this connection.[51]

Mannheim had counted heavily on what he took to be affinities between his work and the developments in America. This relegation to dismissive treatment by fellow-refugees must have been deeply painful. American sociologists have in some measure vindicated Mannheim's more hopeful expectations during the almost fifty years which have elapsed since; but that came too late to influence Mannheim's intellectual agenda or design.

The reviewer in the English *Sociological Review*, Charles H. Wilson, takes up Mannheim's presentation of the work as a collection of essays. He attacks the disclaimer. It puts criticism 'out of court', he protests, and imposes a major and unfair 'disability' on the critic, 'for it inevitably makes the critic feel that he may be in error, and unjust, in imputing to the author this or that fundamental omission, this or that inadequacy of information, this or that contradiction'. 'In fact,' he concludes, 'by this method the author has all the best of it; he all but removes the ground from the reviewer's feet.' But Wilson, a student of Ginsberg, does not appear to have been much cowed.[52] He credits Mannheim with having raised interesting questions about historical relativism and with proposing a useful undertaking, in the analysis of social myths, but he denies that Mannheim has initiated a properly scientific approach to his problems and charges him with eclecticism and inconsistency on the key issues of relativism. Mannheim offers attractive 'speculative generalizations' of the sort which enhance the aesthetic and philosophic interest of the past, he maintains, but nothing to encourage belief that the knowledge of his intellectuals can provide 'scientific, exact, precise diagnosis of cultures'.

MANNHEIM AND BRITISH SOCIAL SCIENCE

Mannheim's attempts to secure recognition of his work from colleagues in his academic discipline, as he had successfully done in Germany, faced great difficulties in England. He judged his peers to be unapproachable by his familiar continental philosophical means, which had, in any case, become problematic for him as well because of the seeming total estrangement between spirit and history. Despite some efforts to cast his theoretical design in terms continuous with traditions of political character study and social psychology deriving from John Stuart Mill, he encountered strong academic resistance or indifference. Appeals to the crisis and to the urgency of strategic experimentation found little resonance within university disciplines.

One connection, however, which Mannheim was able to make fairly early was with a mixed group of university teachers and publicists strongly influenced by British positivist traditions, and Mannheim contributed to an anthology called *Human Affairs* published by them in 1938.[53] In the autobiographical sketch appended to the volume, Mannheim introduces himself in the following way:

> Professor Mannheim's studies commenced with History, Literature, and Philosophy. During the post-war period he gradually realized that a satisfactory explanation of changes in human culture could only be obtained through an exhaustive study of society. For this study of society he took as his guide the sociologist Max Weber. . . . Professor Mannheim's stay in this country has brought home to him

at once the urgent need and the great difficulty of translating one culture in terms of another. The best elements in English and German culture, he holds, need to be synthesized. Neither the purely factual approach of he former nor the purely theoretical approach of the latter is in the long run fruitful; the requirement is an integration of both.[54]

Mannheim's repeated assertions that British sociology is altogether devoid of theoretical traditions signal a fundamental misunderstanding of its history and controversies. This misunderstanding is especially puzzling since it brought him into direct and avoidable conflict with his colleague, Morris Ginsberg, whose opposition destroyed Mannheim's hopes of helping to 'establish sociology'. Mannheim enjoyed increasing popularity as lecturer among students and publics of socially concerned professionals, and many of his English publications had their origins in such lectures, but, as he wrote Wirth in 1938, he thought himself unable to get 'intellectual support' from his peers. In contrast to America, he complains,

> here, it is necessary to quarrel too much with those who are afraid to look new knowledge in the face and to re-learn. This applies above all to my colleague [Morris Ginsberg] . . . who even wanted to get rid of me, out of fear for his way of pursuing a sociology distant from life.[55]

Ginsberg's own indications of his objections to Mannheim's work, however, add up to the contention that Mannheim was reproducing the worst faults of the vague, speculative, and moralizing sociologism which had predominated in the actual history of sociology in Britain.[56]

The tensions between them are manifest in the published records of several conferences in the mid-1930s, which actually had a good deal to do with energetic efforts to 'establish sociology' in Britain on a new, academically respectable level. The British Sociological Society had been the first such society in the world, having been founded in 1903 at a conference addressed by Emile Durkheim, but the discipline had not taken hold in most of the universities. Among the founders were Leonard Hobhouse, Patrick Geddes, and Victor Branford, the first two, ingenious innovators with primary interest in problems of social and political improvement, and the latter, a wealthy and intelligent enthusiast. In addition to the Chair endowed for Hobhouse at the London School of Economics, institutional continuity derived from the Institute of

Sociology and the *Sociological Review*, subsidized and in effect controlled by Victor and Sybella Branford.

By the time Mannheim came to England, the Branfords had
been succeeded by Alexander Farquharson and his wife. 'They were
passionate admirers of Geddes and Branford,' T. H. Marshall has
recalled, 'and yet anxious to stand well with the "academics" of
London University.'[57] The tradition of Geddes and Branford now
appeared as a practice of fieldwork and social surveys, initiated by
Geddes in implementation of the speculative design he derived from
Frederic LePlay, a follower of Auguste Comte. Mannheim criticized
the emphasis on local social descriptions in British sociology,
assimilating it to the untheoretical empiricism he had identified as
the core of American sociology (with regard to which he also came
very late to awareness of the theoretical background), but he seemed
unaware of the theoretical correlate to this work. Yet Mannheim's
conceptions must have sounded oddly and uncomfortably familiar
to some social scientists raised up on Branford's call for a 'third
party' or 'third alternative' between capitalism and socialism, with
the 'town planning' of Geddes as a central feature. Despite the dated
language of 'spirit' and 'evolution', every page of Branford brings
anticipations of Mannheim even to a casual reader. Given Mannheim's links to the pre-war progressivism of Jászi, this can occasion
no surprise, since most of the early British sociologists belonged to
the same general movement of 'the new sociology and the new liberalism'.[58]

Neither Geddes nor Branford appear at all in *Man and Society* or
Diagnosis of Our Time, and Hobhouse comes in only twice, as after-
thought in footnotes devoted to continental thinkers. Mannheim
seemed unaware of the problem and of the consequent need to distinguish his own position from this earlier tradition which Ginsberg
and his associates meant to supersede. A central opportunity would
have been the conferences on the social sciences held in 1935 and the
next two years. Marshall reports:

> After Hobhouse's death (the Farquharsons) won effective
> control of the Institute of Sociology and its Journal and
> were also running the LePlay Society and its field studies
> (which had also been endowed by Branford). So they had
> important facilities to offer to those who wanted to restore
> the quality enjoyed by the early Sociological Society and
> its Papers. Consequently the 'academics' made their move
> to gain control of the *Journal* and to dominate the

academic activities of the Institute without ousting the Farquharsons. The three Conferences of 1935–7 were an important part of this campaign.[59]

The first of these conferences took place in September of 1935. It was called, 'The Social Sciences: Their Relations in Theory and Teaching', and it was opened by an address on 'Sociology Today' by the elderly J. A. Hobson and by a revealing survey on the state of social science, social studies, or sociology as a field of study in British universities, delivered by T. H. Marshall. There is a major in sociology at London University and a field of specialization within the London School of Economics degree, Marshall observes, but that is all, as far degree-level study is concerned. Interdisciplinary social science study is distrusted by most specialists and prevalent only in pre-degree programmes preparing for social work.

> We also notice that the most ambitious schemes of comprehensive social study flourish where the general standard of scholarship is elementary. The prevalence of this policy suggests that experience has confirmed the view that the best education for the less scholarly minds is found in a stimulating contact with a wide range of general ideas.[60]

But this is clearly not what Ginsberg and the other 'academic' sociologists have in mind.

Mannheim's talk, on 'The Place of Sociology',[61] pleads for recognition of sociology as 'the basic discipline of the social sciences', aggressively insists on an analogy with the place of biology in the medical sciences, and characterizes the aim of sociology as 'a complete theory of the totality of the social process'. Early thinkers speculated prematurely, and modern writers fail if they do not have a 'methodological basis', clear concepts, and 'the picture of the totality of the social process constantly before us'. Max Weber's accomplishments show that the time for sociology is ripe. Mannheim then distinguishes among three 'functions' of sociology, the 'systematic', 'comparative' and 'structural'. The distinction between the first two is not clearly drawn, as he associates the phenomenological methods which had originally attracted him to the first with the empirical generalizations which had in earlier years made him so sceptical of the second. The account of structural sociology divides it into social statics and social dynamics, quite in the manner of Comte and John Stuart Mill. His examples are interestingly conservative: he illustrates social statics by an account of elite controls over passive masses, and social dynamics by the disruptive effects of excessive individualistic striving for advancement, as a function of competition.

Ginsberg's remarks on the same subject are not expressly critical of Mannheim. His only substantial reference to him, in fact, is correct and even complimentary. But his presentation as a whole is nevertheless a reproach to Mannheim. He begins by distinguishing between ideal statements about sociology and an empirical account of what sociologists have actually done. While both have their uses, he maintains, the former sometimes leads to needless confusion. When general statements are made about tendencies towards sociology in other sciences, for example, it is helpful to recall that both Hobhouse and Westermarck had already spoken of political science as a branch of sociology in their inaugural addresses in 1907. Then Ginsberg wants to narrow down the precise domain of the discipline, and he rejects the broad claims by Simmel and Vierkandt to have *a priori* systems of all social relations. The 'systematic sociology' discussed by Mannheim can be nothing more than some general statements of findings in comparative sociology; claims made on behalf of the 'direct inspection' characteristic of 'phenomenological method' simply testify to the backward state of social psychology. Although Ginsberg cannot see how anyone can resist Mannheim's 'illuminating' case for a synthetic structural sociology, he remarks, somewhat drily, that such learned commentators as Marshall and Sidgwick had nevertheless recently raised interesting questions, as did others when Hobhouse and Durkheim were first making such claims, based on Comte, in 1903. Ginsberg applies only the second of the two tests which Sidgwick proposes, enquiring whether there is a sufficient measure of 'consensus' between sociologists as different as Hobhouse and Durkheim to warrant the contention that they are at work on a common enterprise. He concludes:

> [At] bottom the trend towards the organic type of society with the pathological deviations from it which Durkheim describes has much in common with the trends towards harmony which Hobhouse seeks to establish with great caution and with many qualifications. Both are concerned with the problem of reconciling individual autonomy and social order and both find the root difficulty in the imperfection of the organic relation so far achieved.[62]

Notwithstanding these similarities, Ginsberg finds an important difference. Unlike Hobhouse, Durkheim had claimed that sociology has its own laws *sui generis*. Without express reference to Mannheim's version of this thesis, Ginsberg coolly urges that any such conclusion be withheld until the study of physiology and psychology is much further advanced.

Any doubts remaining that such statements are to remind audiences that the issues so dramatically promulgated by Mannheim as novelties are in fact long-standing problems, quite well known in England and more carefully developed by others, are dispelled by Ginsberg's contribution to the conference the year after. He chooses as his theme 'Rational and Irrational Elements in Human Behaviour', which also was the topic of Mannheim's just published Hobhouse Lecture, and he opens with the observation that 'the terms "rational" and "irrational" are used in a bewildering variety of senses, due probably to the lack of any generally accepted theory of the nature of value judgements'. For Ginsberg, the concepts themselves belong to social philosophy, with 'rational action' ultimately equivalent to 'right action'. Ginsberg says that it is

> action which is likely on the best available knowledge to satisfy human needs when these are brought clearly to consciousness and examined fairly and impartially with reference to all relevant claims and to the means available for their realisation.

The questions for social scientists, then, centre on the 'psychology of moral life', and especially on 'the reality of moral progress and the part played by reason in it'.[63] The contrast with Mannheim's theses about the crisis of 'substantive rationality' brought about in part by the advance of 'instrumental rationality', could not be more stark.

Mannheim had not been scheduled to speak at this conference. He remarks, however, that he had been asked 'on the eve of the last session to take up some of the threads of the discussion', an assignment he shared with T. H. Marshall. Mannheim undertakes to offer 'a few concrete examples concerning the sociological nature of human valuations, with some theoretical remarks on the difference between the psychological and sociological approach'. This time, it is his turn to be in a position to comment on the 'illuminating remarks' of his colleague. But Mannheim does not address Ginsberg's distinction between the philosophical and sociological aspects of the problem, although this is an issue especially important to Ginsberg and other English thinkers of the time. He turns instead to reflections on examples of uniform contrasts between the values of fighting and sedentary groups, citing research by Ginsberg, among others. He then stops for one of his homilies on method, superfluous and perhaps provocative under the circumstances, since the issues addressed in that research are theoretical. He notes that while 'field observation' is certainly a welcome improvement on 'empty arm-chair speculation', there is, lamentably,

> in this country a tendency to put a premium on pure description, surveys, collections of statistical data, to the exclusion of theoretical and historical analysis of soci-ety. . . . [To] learn from history, we must be able to theor-ise; otherwise the historical facts mean nothing and cannot even be compared or adequately related.

After listing some very general hypotheses about the relationships between valuations and social factors, he closes with a reflection on the contrasts between psychological and sociological approaches. He concludes that psychology studies spontaneous expressions of individual drives, and sociology the counteracting constraints struc-tured by 'established relationships', which are to be understood in terms of their objective functions for society. Instead of explaining why the actions involved in the counteracting constraints may not also be seen as expressions of the subjective impulses of those carry-ing them into effect, he closes with an example which testifies, even over the distance of fifty years, to a rather strained atmosphere in the hall. A psychologist, he says, would study 'the subjective motives which have induced me to waste so much of your time', and he would doubtless come upon 'the subjective urge to self-display'. The sociologist, in contrast, would emphasize the restraining influence of the chairman, who embodies institutionalized arrangements to meet the needs arising out of the scarcity of time. Before an audience of English academics, that disarming gesture, coming at the end of a very long impromptu intervention, may have failed to be helpful.

NOTES

[1]   Mannheim Papers, University of Keele.
[2]   *Ibid.*, October 1933.
[3]   'Persverslag van den Universitairen leergang gehouden van 12–27 September 1933', *Algemeen Nederlandsch Tijdschrift voor Wijsbegeerte en Phsychologie* **27** (January 1934), p. 39.
[4]   Neither the text nor a detailed report of this material has been located, but the descriptive paragraphs in German, printed in

the course announcement and probably drafted by the lecturers themselves, make it highly likely that Mannheim's lecture was a preliminary version of the material he published in the following year in the Netherlands as Part III of *Mensch und Gesellschaft im Zeitalter des Umbaus*.

[5]   *Man and Society in an Age of Reconstruction* (London: Routledge & Kegan Paul, 1940), p. 223.

[6]   *Ibid.*, pp. 212f.

[7]   *Ibid.*, p. 222.

[8]   *Ibid.*

[9]   *Ibid.*, p. 228.

[10] *Ibid.*, p. 188.

[11] John Stuart Mill, *A System of Logic*, 8th edn., (Philadelphia: Harper and Brothers, 1881), pp. 599, 640. It should be noted that Mill never uses the Latin expression which Mannheim favors, '*principia media*'; he says '*axiomata media*' or uses the English. But Mannheim's citation of Mill leaves no doubt that he is referring to at least the former of these passages.

[12] *Ibid.*, p. 656.

[13] *Man and Society*, p. 236.

[14] *Ibid.*, p. 177.

[15] *Ibid.*, p. 178.

[16] See David Kettler, 'Sociology of Knowledge and Moral Philosophy: The Place of Traditional Problems in the Formation of Mannheim's Thought', *Political Science Quarterly*, Vol. 82, 3 (September 1967).

[17] *Ideologie und Utopie*, 3rd edn (Frankfurt am Main: Schulte-Bulmke, 1952), p. 93.

[18] 'Die geistige Krise im Lichte der Soziologie', *Stuttgarter Neues Tageblatt* (December 31, 1932).

[19] *Ibid.*

[20] *Sociological Review* **26**, 2 (April 1934), pp. 105ff.

[21] 'A Syllabus on Power', prepared for the Moot, January 1943. Reproduced in Charles Cooper's unpublished typescript, *The Hindu Prince: A Sociological Biography of Karl Mannheim*.

[22] Letter to Oscar Jászi, November 8, 1936, *loc. cit.*

[23] *Man and Society*, pp. 74–5.

[24] *Ibid.*, pp. 97–8.

[25] *Ibid.*, p. 193.

[26] *Ibid.*, p. 193.

[27] *Ibid.*, pp. 198f.

[28] *Ibid.*, p. 346.

[29] Nicholaus Sombart, 'Henri de Saint-Simon und Auguste Comte', in Alfred Weber, ed., *Einführung in die Soziologie* (Munich: Pieper, 1955), pp. 88f.

[30] *Man and Society*, pp. 147–8.

[31] *Ibid*., pp. 3–6.

[32] *Ibid*., pp. 14–15.

[33] *Ibid*., pp. 32–33.

[34] *Ibid*., p. 27.

[35] Review of Ernst Cassirer, *Freiheit und Form: Studien zur deutschen Geistesgeschichte*, in *Athenaeum* (Budapest), **3**(1917), p. 409.

[36] Letter to Louis Wirth of November 17th, 1930, University of Chicago, Joseph Regenstein Library, Archives, Louis Wirth Papers.

[37] Ernst Robert Curtius, 'Soziologie – und ihre Grenzen', *Neue Schweizer Rundschau*, **33** (October 1929), pp. 727–736. Reprinted in Volker Meja and Nico Stehr, *Der Streit um die Wissenssoziologie*, Vol. 2, pp. 417–426.

[38] Letter to Louis Wirth of November 17th, 1930. According to T. H. Marshall, who was Mannheim's colleague at the London School of Economics, Mannheim never fully understood that the appointment was one of those funded by a special collection among the faculty, organized by Lionel Robbins and Lord Beveridge, and not seen as permanent or entitling the holders to full participation in collegial academic decisions. (Personal interview with Professor Marshall in September 1976.) See also Lord Beveridge, *The London School of Economics and its Problems, 1919–1937* (London: George Allen & Unwin, 1960), p. 236.

[39] In *Essays on the Sociology of Culture*, ed. Ernst Mannheim in cooperation with Paul Kecskemeti (London: Routledge & Kegan Paul, 1956), pp. 15–89. The editors' remarks and the evidence of the texts of the volume indicate that changes were made in the manuscripts after Mannheim's death. Since the originals upon which the posthumous publications were based no longer appear to be available, we have decided not to use these sources, except when their main principles and methods are well supported by other materials. Much the same can be said about *Freedom, Power, and Democratic Planning*, also published posthumously and reported by a well qualified witness to be different from the last draft he saw in Mannheim's hands. The reconstructions freely adapted from lecture notes and published as *Systematic Sociology* and *Sociology*

of Education also cannot be of use in the present investigation. This is not to suggest any impropriety or incompetence in these attempts to distil and assemble 'ideas' from Mannheim. The approach followed here, because of its interest in Mannheim's essayistic method and the connections between form and content in his work, make special demands, however.

[40] *Man and Society*, pp. 365f.
[41] Morris Ginsberg, 'Recent Tendencies in Sociology', reprinted as chapter five of *Reason and Unreason in Society* (Cambridge, Mass.: Harvard University Press, 1948), p. 121.
[42] Ginsberg, 'The Place of Sociology', in *The Social Sciences: Their Relations in Theory and in Teaching* (London: LePlay House Press, 1936), p. 125.
[43] Personal interviews with Edward Shils (August 23, 1967) and Jean Floud (March 2, 1976). Cf. also Joseph Gabel, 'Mannheim et le marxisme hongrois', *L'homme et la societé*, (January–March 1969), pp. 127–146. Professor Gabel's thesis, that the Americans shifted Mannheim's work away from Mannheim's own preoccupations with 'political consciousness' towards an American indifference to the distinction between true and false consciousness and a consequent threat to the distinction between ideology and knowledge as well, is an ingenious inference from the information available to him. The historical record speaks unambiguously against it, however.
[44] Letter to Wirth of December 24, 1935.
[45] Wirth to Mannheim, February 2, 1936.
[46] Mannheim to Wirth, February 15, 1936.
[47] *Ibid.*
[48] Cf. *Ideologie und Utopie*, p. 85, and *Ideology and Utopia* p. 86.
[49] *Ideologie und Utopie*, p. 159.
[50] Mannheim to Wirth on December 28, 1936.
[51] Mannheim to Wirth on July 3, 1937.
[52] *Sociological Review*, **29**, 4 (October 1937), pp. 414–419.
[53] R. B. Cattell, J. I. Cohen, and R. M. W. Travers, eds, *Human Affairs* (London: Macmillan, 1937). Mannheim's contribution is a draft of what was to become Part V of *Man and Society*, here called 'Present Trends in the Building of Society', pp. 278–300. The contributors include J. B. S. Haldane, Lord Raglan, Havelock Ellis, B. Malinowski, William McDougall and Morris Ginsberg.
[54] *Ibid.*, p. 355.

[55] Mannheim to Wirth on August 13, 1938.

[56] If the intensity of his reactions in an interview twenty-five years after the event are any guide, Ginsberg became very hostile to Mannheim. In his later recollections, he put special emphasis on what he considered to have been Mannheim's facile popularizations, which attracted large numbers of undergraduate students, overstimulated them with vast and portentous questions, and left them with no analytical method for doing social research or philosophical reflection, especially since Mannheim failed to distinguish between sociology and social philosophy. It should be said, to the credit of both eminent sociologists, that their students were given no sign of the conflict between them, according to the authoritative testimony of Jean Floud, a student of Ginsberg, who was working as Mannheim's unpaid assistant during the revision of *Ideology and Utopia* and also assisted on *Man and Society*.

[57] Personal interview with T. H. Marshall, September 1976.

[58] Philip Abrams, *The Origins of British Sociology*, 1834–1914. (Chicago and London: The University of Chicago Press, 1968), p. 60. For an authentic overview of Branford, see Sybella Gurney Branford's review essay of Victor Branford's *Science and Sanctity* in *Sociological Review*, **19**:4 (October 1927), pp. 335ff.

[59] Personal interview with T. H. Marshall, September 1976.

[60] T. H. Marshall, 'Report on the Teaching of the Social Sciences', *The Social Sciences*, loc. cit., p. 40.

[61] *Ibid.*, pp. 164ff.

[62] *Ibid.*, p. 205.

[63] In J. E. Dugdale, ed., *Further Papers on the Social Sciences: Their Relations in Theory and in Teaching* (London: LePlay House Press, 1937), p. 117.

4

Towards a Rational Society?

THE 'MOOT': MANNHEIM AND THE ORGANIZATION OF AN ELITE

Mannheim's method depends on the reception of his diagnosis and therapeutic proposals as timely and relevant. While his social scientific reference group in Britain remained sceptical, Mannheim enjoyed increasing success in a different forum. His final design for rational incorporation of irrational social tendencies reflects this new connection.

In the same letter to Wirth in which he reported on the quarrel arising out of Ginsberg's presumed 'fear' of looking 'new knowledge in the face' and his inability to 'relearn', Mannheim also writes:

> There are symptoms that reveal that the way of comprehending and interpreting culture which you and I represent has been taken note of by very influential English circles. I do not view it as an illusion, that in connection with the renaissance of democratic nations in the campaign against Fascism, this will play a role quite soon.[1]

A few months later Mannheim is quite elated:

> Life in London is very delightful – the English are chang-
> ing rapidly. The dynamism of the time reminds me a little
> of the Weimar Republic, as is also shown by the growth of
> my following among students and the general public. One
> has the feeling of having a 'mission'.[2]

This theme of 'mission,', reminiscent of Mannheim's earlier 'feeling
or illusion that one is needed' for the 'task' of 'establishing sociology', now refers to action on a wider stage. He writes, just after the
outbreak of war:

> I feel, however sad the happenings are, it is our hour, and
> our study of society which formerly perhaps had been the
> satisfaction of scientific curiosity or pleasure in profes-
> sional skill, must become the tool of the surgeon.[3]

Despite the tone of expectation, the letter must also report that
the Director of the London School of Economics has encouraged him
to go through with the planned trip to America and to make use of
the opportunity by finding some employment there, since he would
not be needed in the reduced wartime programme Mannheim speculates that there may well be some financial reasons for this advice
but that it doubtless also arises out of 'the wish that the time of war
should be used by those who, like me, have connections in America,
for building bridges and making contacts between England and the
USA.' Later in the letter, having enquired about prospects for temporary employment, he escalates his speculations:

> If I come to America it is very likely that I should be
> charged with the task of fostering cooperation between
> scholars and exponents of public opinion.

Nothing came of these American plans, and Mannheim spent
the war-years in various locations with the evacuated London
School of Economics, working part-time, and then with the Institute
of Education of the University of London, where he had a regular
chair. He did in fact establish himself during those years as representative from one world to another, although not in the sense he
had expected. His 'mission', as it turned out, made him spokesman
for secular, sociological thinking within the association of clerical
and lay figures grouped around a prominent Christian publicist,
organizer, and noted missionary, J. H. Oldham. In this setting, his
legitimacy as sociologist was never challenged; but neither could it
be tested and affirmed.

A close associate of William Temple, Archbishop of Canterbury, Oldham had become convinced, according to Temple's biographer.

> that the most serious danger to the Christian Faith lay . . . in the secularism which was clearly defined by the trend of political organization and social thinking in the years between the two wars. . . . [T]otalitarianism and 'scientific' humanism [now] . . . constituted the dominant creeds in State and Community. Here were two weapons pointed straight at the heart of the Christian Faith and The Christian Way of Life.[4]

To propagate the Christian social thought generated by the Oxford Conference on 'Church, Community, and State', Oldham sought to found something he called an 'order', to advance the cause of a Christian society with more initiative and intensity than could be expected from formal Church organizations, and with access to expert advice.

Mannheim was not present during the long weekend in April of 1938, when Oldham first brought together the group whose counsel and support he wanted and which styled itself the 'Moot'. But he joined at the next meeting, in September of that year, and he is the only member except Oldham who was present on all eighteen occasions for which records were kept. There were twenty-four meetings in all, and the organization dissolved a few days after Mannheim's death on January 10, 1947. In addition to Oldham and Mannheim, the group included a number of prominent clergymen, T. S. Eliot, Adolph Löwe (until his move to Manchester in 1940), Professor H. A. Hodges, John Middleton Murry, and Sir Fred Clarke, the director of the Institute of Education, where Mannheim was to be called to teach. The formal activity of the Moot was limited to periodic meetings to discuss books or papers submitted by members or invited guests, usually after preliminary written exchanges among the most interested of the participants. But the group also generated the *Christian News-Letter*, which had a circulation of 10,000 and was edited by Oldham together with others in the group, a series of *Christian News-Letter* books, mostly on education, a series of lunches which brough a larger circle of public figures together with members of the group, under the name of the 'Christian Frontier Council', and numerous local branches and offshoots, like the one organized by A. D. Lindsay, the Master of Balliol, at Oxford, in which Mannheim also evidently played a part. Through these extensions of the

Moot network, Mannheim became close to Lindsay, Zimmern, and other established university people, in a wide variety of fields, but sharing an interest in social reform and adult education, under Christian auspices. Mannheim appears to have been the most frequent contributor of papers to the Moot and the most regular circulator of memoranda, and virtually every publication after he became a member originated in some sort of presentation to this group.

Mannheim's first contribution came at the second Moot which he attended, when he read 'Planning for Freedom', which was later expanded to become Part Five of *Man and Society in an Age of Reconstruction*. This was to be Mannheim's definitive restatement of the position towards which the first few essays after 1933 are working. But equally significant for an understanding of Mannheim's adaptation of his design for his new audience is a memorandum which he distributed in preparation for the second topic of the weekend, on *True Humanism*, by Jacques Maritain, a liberal democratic Catholic thinker. Mannheim's criticism of Maritain indicates his conception of the group and of his role within it. They also suggest an important readjustment in his conception of his own 'way to knowledge'. Claims of sweeping authority for science as the element of reason amidst the universal crisis of irrationality give way to the image of the sociologist as 'practical thinker', as counsellor and partner to an elite loyal to traditional values. Mannheim speaks of 'our problems' and 'our philosophy' with a new confidence and concreteness of reference; he sees himself allied with a real force against a 'concrete enemy'. He is not simply an adviser on problems of implementation, however broadly conceived; he is proposing to become a collaborator in the composition of a ' "*Summa*" for our age'. This can only be done, he maintains, by 'linking up the philosophical and ontological approach . . . with the empirical and instrumental one'; and this requires, in turn, 'a closer cooperation between the philosopher, the theologian, and the practical thinker'.[5]

A letter to Oldham several years later [6] indicates that the talk of a '*Summa*' had not been merely a passing reference occasioned by Maritain's devotion to St Thomas Aquinas. It also indicates what Mannheim understood by the term:

> I am glad to see that my suggestion for working out a '*Summa*' has been supported by M. Murray and you. May I now add another suggestion? The discussion of a '*Summa*' as such may lead to an over-abstract discussion

of pure principles. Would it not be better, as it is our aim
that our proposals should be in the spirit of Christianity,
that we should start with the discussion of . . . [the] surveys [I have proposed] concerning the recent changes in
society. This would automatically lead us back to the discussion of the underlying principles of our proposals. Thus
the meaning of the Christian attitude to the present world
[the main content of a new '*Summa*'] would directly grow
out of our discussion of the concrete details.[7]

The '*Summa*' and the practical advice are inwardly connected. A
'*Summa*', Mannheim contends, serves 'to bring our philosophy
closer to the world of everyday affairs and the outlook of the empirical thinker'.[8] Empirical and instrumental thinking cannot itself
create such a comprehensive knowledge. But they are the starting
point.

Mannheim's comments on Maritain anticipate this view. Maritain's humanism is too abstract, he objects, too much concerned
with what some others may have thought and not enough with what
has happened and what must be done:

Maritain's book would be even more topical and might be
a prelude to action if he had had a concrete enemy such as
the Communist, Fascist or Liberal in mind. . . . He could
not in that case have avoided a discussion of the strategy of
action which would have led him to a more thorough
analysis both of the social setting and the actual psychology of the people to be changed.[9]

Bonds between social thinking, social action, and 'topicality', – i.e.
belonging to a place – are familiar elements in Mannheim's thinking, and there are clear similarities between this general approach
and what Mannheim had called 'thinking out of a situation' in his
early work, and '*Lebenswissenschaftliche Methode*' in his Frankfurt university lectures. But it is nevertheless striking to see how earlier
'dialectical' paradoxes of 'homelessness', 'relative social detachment', and 'unplanned planners' give way to the security of shared
English identity, mobilizing against 'concrete enemies' under the
traditional symbols of Church and State. Among Mannheim's earlier conceptions, it most resembles the interplay between socially
mobile intellectuals and place-bound anti-modern classes which
Mannheim had examined years before in his work on German conservatism. As in that case, despite the seeming harmonious adjust-

ment, paradoxes abound. Mannheim is aware of himself as 'refugee' among those who belong: he remained a Jew among Christians; he was a secularist among the faithful; and he continued to aspire to a theoretical completeness which was belied by the regimen of topical and occasional pieces to which, despite all talk of a *'Summa'*, he now seemed committed.

After Mannheim's death in 1947, the *Times* obituary said that 'in a remarkably short time he penetrated to the essence of the English spirit, and became, in some ways, more English than the English themselves'.[10] It is neither a denial of the sincerity of the tribute nor an affront to Mannheim's deserved reputation to notice that these two clauses add up to an ironic awareness of Mannheim's strenuous effort to bridge what may not have been bridgeable. 'Essence of the English spirit' is an expression after Mannheim himself; 'more English than the English' is an English comment on it.

Like his turn towards sociological professionalism in the late 1920s, Mannheim's commitment to the network of English social Christianity had more than careerist purposes and did not imply abandonment of his own distinctive project. Here was another of his 'experiments', doubtless undertaken with that modern personal self-awareness which he found in such 'experimental' lives as that of Saint-Simon. He was on a 'mission' among these missionaries. Yet the experiment was not altogether successful. He had once memorialized Ernst Troeltsch as having sacrificed his 'inwardness' in order to mediate between the academic and the public worlds. Mannheim paid a similarly heavy price during those late years. He suspended theoretical reflectivity, the main strength of his best work. When he finally formulated a comprehensive statement of the political creed he regarded as the adequate contemporary expression of liberalism, he practically abandoned the claim to characterize and justify it as a structure of knowledge. The quest begun in the tension between Jászi and Lukács – mirroring the one which John Stuart Mill had begun three generations earlier, between Bentham and Coleridge – ended prematurely, in exhortation.

This unfortunate aspect of Mannheim's position comes out especially clearly in two encounters with Michael Polanyi, upon whom Mannheim's legitimations as refugee or as scientist could make no impression. Polanyi had been Karl Mannheim's contemporary in Budapest. He had been less active in the radical intellectual life of the time than his brother, Karl, but both were Christian believers and attained scholarly prominence. In the 1930s, Polanyi was well established as a chemist in Britain, and he was also gaining recognition for his philosophical reflections on the personal dimension in scientific work. According to the recollection of a participant, Polanyi's visit to the Moot in 1944 occasioned 'a ding-dong battle between Polanyi and Mannheim, the latter being taken by surprise at Polanyi's demonstration of the intuitive and traditional elements in all scientific discovery'.[11] This report is confirmed and given wider significance by an exchange of letters between Mannheim and Polanyi.

Polanyi writes to thank Mannheim for an evening's entertainment, their first long talk since Budapest, and he confirms plans for the book which Mannheim has offered to include in the 'International Library of Sociology and Social Reconstruction'. Then Polanyi expresses some annoyance that Mannheim has seen fit to cross-question him on the sources and origins of his religious convictions, as if they were some sort of pathological symptom. Polanyi rejects categorically any thought that his beliefs could be explained as functions of psychological or sociological factors:

> I reject all social analysis of history which makes social conditions anything more than *opportunities* for a development of thought. You seem inclined to consider moral judgements on history as ludicrous, believing apparently that thought is not merely conditioned, but determined by a social or technical situation. I cannot tell you how strongly I reject such a view.[12]

Mannheim replies soothingly, but expresses surprise that a scientist would make categorical judgements about something that is after all an empirical question, and he asks:

> What would happen in science if one were still to go on to do what one did with Galileo, to reject factual statements because they were in contradiction with some religious or moral axiom one happened to hold?[13]

Polanyi does not accept this commonplace. In a homely illustration of Kantian fundamentals, he says that every time he comes to his laboratory, he must draw on his reserves of categorical confidence in the logic of science, since the experiments left in the charge of his collaborators and assistants may all have failed.

> Failures prevail overwhelmingly over successes, and the lack of reproducibility of phenomena is our daily bitter experience. . . . Still, from all this experience we do not

draw the conclusion that natural events are governed by
magic or by the devil – even though everything points in
that direction.

When it comes to history, he asserts, we must also make assumptions in order to understand anything at all, only now these assumptions are about moral and intellectual freedom and responsibility.

No life can be without some conviction and the necessity to
embrace one is as irresistible to the normal intelligence as
it is to our normal moral instincts. So there is no way out.
We must choose – and usually we have chosen already by
implication. That is, we must choose in such a fashion that
what we instinctively love in life, what we spontaneously
admire, what we irresistibly aspire to, should make sense
in the light of our convictions. When the prospect of such a
solution opens up before our eyes, we undergo a conversion. Henceforth we do not doubt the faith to which we have
been converted, but rather reject such evidence as may seem
to contradict it. By exposing the fallaciousness of such evidence we fulfil our daily task and find ever renewed confirmation for our fundamental beliefs.[14]

What is striking about the exchanges is, first, that Mannheim
puts himself in a false dogmatic position about science, drastically at
variance with what he knows about the problems, and, second, that
he addresses sceptical questions about religion to a compatriot,
although he would have been too prudent to raise them at the Moot.
Both points give rise to misgivings about the extent to which Mannheim's experiments in identity jeopardized his critical powers and
intellectual integrity. The question arises whether Mannheim made a
'*sacrifice quotidien*' for the sake of securing what Marx once called 'the
this-sidedness of thinking', even as his erstwhile mentor Georg
Lukács did within the Stalinist Communist Party.[15]

Such analyses are suggestive and troubling, but they are nevertheless misleading in decisive respects. The founders of the Moot
shared a certain general orientation, including a sense that they
must somehow come closer to action, but they were hardly inclined
to exercise overt intellectual controls and little equipped for political
mobilization. At most, it can be said that some of them dimly
thought they ought to display more of these qualities and that
occasionally they had a regrettable weakness for expressing these
vague aspirations by wishing for a Christian counterpart to *Mein
Kampf* and for mastery of the successful techniques of the Nazi

movement. For Mannheim, acceptance by the Moot represented a valued and tempting opportunity rather than submission to a creed or organization.

Unlike the academic practitioners of social science disciplines, whom Mannheim found impartially indifferent to his warnings of systemic dissolution and projections of total regeneration, these Christians had a sense of 'crisis'. But they naturally tended to think of the 'crisis' as a 'spiritual' one, in the senses common to well-established Christian churches, and Mannheim accordingly often began his diagnoses with a notion of a 'crisis in valuation' rather than a 'crisis in rationality'. In terms of the sociological tradition, this turned his thoughts more in the direction of Durkheim and the need to overcome *anomie* than towards Max Weber's rich ambivalences about rationalization or Marx's developmental sequences. But this was simply an added impetus to Mannheim's already evident redefinition of the central therapeutic task as one of finding more adequate replacements for the processes of the division of labour, professionalization, and legalization, which Durkheim had seen as constitutive of modern organic integration. Now, however, the sociologically abstract 'planner', to whom Mannheim assigned a central part in this alternate constitutional process, could be associated with an historical type combining theory and practice in a way not available elsewhere.

Mannheim's notes for a major study of intellectuals, which he never published, contain many pages on the type of the 'gentleman', and he thought that the historical emergence on this type in England, in conjunction with the special character of the 'professional man' and the 'civil servant', prevented the formation of an 'intelligentsia' in the continental sense and alleviated the dilemmas of relating theory and practice. Although averse to abstruse speculation, the gentleman recognizes that 'knowledge is power', according to Mannheim, and accepts it as his obligation to put his knowledge at the service of the public. In the terms of his earlier diagnoses of the multiple crises of modernity, this means that the crisis of mass democratization has been muted in England by structural rather than accidental historical factors: 'Mass democracy' is countered by an unusually successful 'democracy of the few'. Accordingly, Mannheim used his influence in educational circles on the side of those resisting democratization of the school system in the post-war plans, and he especially protected the public schools. More generally, the task which Mannheim had earlier defined as bringing intellectuals to self-consciousness now appears as subjecting gentlemen to organization, revising the instrumental knowledge and forms of power at their disposal, while confident that they are in a position to recognize and utilize both. This notion of bringing 'gentlemen' to see themselves as destined for a planning elite, Mannheim believes, overcomes the paradoxes involved in bringing intellectuals to power.

Mannheim contends that past performance and future prospects of this elite make it unnecessary to interfere with the conventionalized institutions of parliamentary democracy. Like the Crown, the forms of parliamentary rule lend legitimacy and continuity to the instrumentalities for social control, even while the substance of decision must be ever more clearly left to processes capable of determined realism, far-sighted planning, universal coordination, and strategic sequential implementation.

The traditional values of England's liberal democracy, moreover, now appear to have substantive worth for the planning process, when properly interpreted. Mannheim finds similarities between traditional conceptions of freedom and his own notion that freedom is an element of spontaneous choice and decision within a structured framework of constraints essential to the freedom itself. Without freedom in this sense, he maintains, planning will not contain the pressures generated by excessive discipline and it will not retain the capacity for innovation. The new social knowledge, in other words, does not have to explode and displace all established social belief, as Saint-Simon and Comte had thought, and as Mannheim himself had earlier experimentally conjectured, but neither does it arise out of a dialectical interplay with contesting social doctrines, as the sociology of a knowledge had once proclaimed. Sociology must inform, revitalize, and concretize the beliefs beyond knowledge upon which traditional values rest, and the reoriented elite must then point its control in new directions.

A critical point to which Mannheim keeps returning during the years of the Moot is the original notion of an 'order'. It was doubtless this notion that persuaded Mannheim that these influential religious gentlemen might be serious about organizing for action, and this made the idea of joining with them in forging a doctrinal 'Summa' intimately connected with wide-ranging and long-term strategy seem so promising. Yet it was also on this point that the most sustained disagreements prevailed within the group. Some of them became manifest at the very first meeting. The Catholic historian, Christopher Dawson, spoke about the ultimate ideal of a 'Christian totalitarianism', and the Cambridge theologian, H. H. Farmer, set up the Nazi Party as a model for the order to be founded, stressing its closeness to everyday issues, its 'transcendence' and its ingenious range of educational methods. T. S. Eliot and Oldham himself cautioned that the order must be kept 'informal' and 'elastic', distinguished by 'friendship' and 'free discussion'.[16] In the following meetings, through the years of the Moot, Mannheim took the lead in urging concrete political tasks and a measure of political organization upon the members. At his first meeting, the Moot agreed in principle to provide for 'staff and cell groups'. Mannheim next proposed that members use their specific institutes and other lines of connection to educate for change. Despite some objections to this emphasis, Oldham was carried away to speak of founding 'something analogous to "The Party" (sic)', though also 'wholly different' from the Nazi or Communist Party. These plans came to nothing and a reduced group decided to keep the Moot in being, but to restrict it to the 'body of friends who have established through common experience a certain relationship and common life'.

The informality projected by this resolution did not dampen Mannheim's expectations or his campaign. In February of 1940, Mannheim presses for 'decisiveness' and an 'active order', urging imitation of a 'revolution from above'. Two months later, he repents somewhat of that expression, but speaks with surprising enthusiasm and insensitivity:

> The Germans, Russians and Italians are more advanced than we are in the techniques of managing modern society, but their purposes are wrong and even atavistic. We may look to elite groups in our society, e.g. the Moot, or enlightened Civil Servants, to use these techniques for different ends. The new techniques constitute a new opportunity and a new obligation.[17]

By April 1940, when these uncritical remarks were made, the Moscow Trials and associated 'techniques' cannot have been unknown to Mannheim and his audience, not to speak of the German administrative measures which had, among other things, brought Mannheim to England. Mannheim was so fixed on the general message he wanted to convey and on the rhetorical opportunities provided by the situation that his judgement became at times quite perverse. His remarks continue:

> We want to mobilize the intelligent people of goodwill in this country who are waiting for a lead. At the same time

there must be a popular movement to back what the elites
are doing. You cannot built up a great movement without
the dynamism of social leadership. I am amazed by our
lethargy.

They were worrying times, and Mannheim doubtless spoke out
of great anxiety, in a company he thought he knew well enough to
stir up with his exasperation. Yet there is an extraordinary lack of
political judgement in all this:

We are always waiting for means. But are not the means
there? e.g., the Christian youth movement which is waiting
for a lead, Oldham's access to people in key positions, the
Christian News-Letter, the BBC, public schools, groups in
the churches, etc. We are too lazy to move. Hitler started
with six people.

One of the members was thereupon moved to produce a 'Bill of
Duties', which Mannheim delightedly proclaimed 'a magnificent
instrument for creating a popular movement'. Nothing more was
heard of it, of course, although Mannheim reproaches Oldham with
neglect of such initiatives for action, in a letter sent three years later.

In a memorandum almost certainly prepared for A. D. Lindsay's Oxford branch of the movement, Mannheim proposes quite a
different approach. He begins with a suprising revision of a
metaphor he cannot have forgotten. Having asserted that 'total war
demands the total mobilization of our intellectual and spiritual
resources', he contends that 'we can afford to wage the battle in the
intellectual field because we have, as a weapon, the social sciences'.[18] (Max Weber, of course, had thought that it was political
ideology that was designed to serve as weapon). Mannheim urges
formation of a new social science faculty to conduct research and
re-educate educators, social workers, and pastors. It would also
train leadership cadres for a youth movement. One of the 'most
urgent tasks' of the research would be to elaborate 'our pattern of
social reconstruction', which 'would become the basis for our foreign
and home propaganda'. While social science education and research
would encourage free discussion, the leadership training would be
different:

It is here that the great mistakes of our pre-war democracy
must be corrected, namely that the intellect of our youth
has been too much severed from action, and that freedom
of discussion was misintegrated as a shameless anarchy of

varying opinions on the basis of which no cooperation could exist. What should be established in these self-governing groups is the elaboration of a discipline, of a code of conduct, which make a pioneering attitude possible.[19]

The contrast with Mannheim's 1929 design for political education is striking. Mannheim's preoccupation with youth also plays a prominent part in the last of his long memoranda on the need for more concerted political program and action in the 'order'. He likens present-day youth to the generation of 1914, stressing their 'activism' and disdain for prudence. He invokes the powerful symbolry of Munich in an altogether unexpected way:

> Opposed to the umbrella is the symbol of the trench-coat which (Hitler) wore with such emphasis. In this struggle . . . what should be our decision? With whom should we side?[20]

The need is to accept this activism and to see that it is 'directed to those issues which we feel to be constructive and creative'.

His last statement on the proposed 'order' offers his most carefully weighed judgement about the relationship between established elites and what he wants the Moot to be. He begins by praising the record of adaptability and innovation of the British 'historical leadership', but finds that a tendency towards oligarchy has reduced their vitality.

> The test . . . is whether in times of emergency they are capable of reorganising themselves from within, breaking traditional habits of mind, revitalising the dynamic elements in their own traditions, making the best use of outward stimuli and of personality types outside the boundaries of their own social groups.

When vitality is lost, change by violent revolution is likely.

> There is only one organic way of preventing deterioration; it is regeneration from within. The regeneration of a group consists in a vital participation in a new spiritual movement by those members of the group who are the most alive.[21]

While isolated individuals have these capacities, they cannot be secure or effective in their exercises unless they mutually reinforce one another.

> The task of the 'Order' is exactly this: that it should draw
> together on terms of fellowship these pioneering minds
> who otherwise would remain inefficient in their isolation.

Vitality depends on incorporation of individuals like himself. Mannheim likens the members of the Moot to the twelve just men of
Jewish legend upon whom the world rests, adding only that they
should organize.

From this Jewish analogy he moves abruptly to the inner circle
of the Communist party in Russia or the Nazi and fascist elites.
There are differences.

> We can do without such rigid regimentation because the
> inner cohesion and solidarity of the leading groups in this
> country is strong enough to guarantee co-ordinated action
> in case of emergency. . . . As long as this country possesses
> a historical leadership which is elastic enough to give a
> lead to social reconstruction, there is no need for the crea-
> tion of a new single-party system.[22]

He claims a functional equivalence between a 'single-party system'
and 'historical leadership' and shows that he attaches little importance to party competition.

The reasonable grounds for the distinctions between parties are
gone. 'Right' and 'Left' have been discredited by the fascists and by
Stalin and 'nobody in the community who identifies himself with the
historical situation in which we are fated to live' could follow this
lead.

> The strategic situation in terms of a historical setting pre-
> pares the ground for cooperation between all those who
> want both to maintain historical values and to bring about
> social reconstruction.[23]

Mannheim's conception of the 'order' attached great significance to
his involvement in the Moot and helps to explain his investment in
its activities.

A testy letter to Oldham in 1943 indicates a measure of disillusionment without acknowledging the effects of mutual misunderstanding. Oldham had circulated a memorandum on 'The Frater-
nity of the Spirit', and Mannheim complains that the Moot was
closer to a commitment to action in 1940. All this talk about pure
'inwardness' and spirituality will itself 'kill the spirit'. 'Nobody who
really means business will join a fellowship in which he cannot know

what his commitment will mean in the concrete situation.' He continues,

> I appreciate . . . the subtlety of this invisible social network as long as its task is the propagation of inner experience only. But I see no justification for this subtlety if our aim is the collection of men to whom ideas mean action.

Mannheim concludes with a sort of valedictory to his disappointed hopes, characteristically ascribed to an objective process in which he simply participated:

> I may perhaps remind you of the fact that the idea of the order was originally conceived in strict connection with the assumption that it might one day become our mission to make this country aware of her opportunity to develop the new pattern of society, which is neither communist nor fascist, which is planned but still preserves the essential forms of freedom and all that on the basis of a pledge between the parties which could spare us the detrimental effect of a revolutionary upheaval. The idea was that if a religious group were to conceive and develop the image of a new order of society, its mediation between the parties would not only help them to overcome their partisan views but also to bring about the necessary sacrifice which is needed if the reconstruction is to be carried out to the benefit of the whole. At the same time it was felt that if ever there was a chance in history for the idea of Christianity really to influence our social institutions it was at the present juncture.[24]

Doubtless Mannheim gained the assent of all or most of the Moot to all or most of these propositions at one time or another. But the Moot was not a centre point for identity or action for most of the others, as it was for Mannheim. Sir Walter Moberly, chairman of the University Grants Committee from 1935 to 1949, said it strikingly, in an ingenuous idiom which the sociologist Mannheim must have found very clear, when he confessed his discomfort about Mannheim's proposal for 'revolution from above':

> The Moot was in part composed of people who had cut themselves loose from ordinary standards of comfort, etc. (and who therefore had a reality of attack lacking in others), and in part of people like himself, who had com-

paratively large stipends and were consequently enmeshed in a certain range of social obligations.[25]

The Moot continued for four years after Mannheim's solemn reproach to Oldham, and Mannheim remained active and respected. But his focus shifted to the Institute of Education and the International Library of Sociology and Social Reconstruction. And he never completed another work for publication.

A POLITICAL SOCIOLOGY

Between the later of the essays in *Man and Society* and the time of his death, Mannheim was at work on a political sociology. It was to be a sociological interpretation of political life, and the interpretation itself was to be an integral and indeed transformative component of that life. He puts aside the immediate, fluctuating power constellations which dictates political tactics as beyond his ken, and addresses the larger situation, requiring a plan, a structured and strategic response. Since he considers the older political theories, as well as the newer political science, as nothing more than partial sociological studies, perspectivistically inhibited from recognition of the inter-dependencies affecting political institutions, he also offers his political sociology as a correction to general political thinking. All human institutions, he writes, 'are permanent elements in the political organization of society'.[26]

The central 'practices and agencies' under examination are those 'which have as their ultimate aim the moulding of human behaviour and of social relationships',[27] and he calls these 'social techniques'. Elsewhere he speaks, although not much more precisely, of the function of 'social control' which achieves the 'socialization' of the human beings present in a certain space and time, integrating them in a system of social cooperation. Adapting Marxist ideas, he maintains that the progressive development of social techniques is the decisive social process, moving society through traditional and liberal stages towards planning. Crisis erupts when new techniques render old ones ineffective without as yet becoming predominant, and it brings the threat and then, suddenly and unexpectedly, the reality of 'chaos'. The strategic political task is to use appropriate social techniques to give full systematic command to the social techniques required by the state of development.

If the political function in general is to be equated to social control, government is the social technique for the control of controls. Liberal parliamentarianism had accomplished this control by providing a forum within which interests could compete, and by legitimating the ensuing compromises by means of legal formalization. The rational legality it produced and the implementing mechanisms it empowered depended on traditional beliefs shared in the political community since the Middle Ages and were not themselves the result of a legislation or adjudication. Liberal government presupposed reinforcement from tradition. The autonomous economic domain was also out of its control; and it constituted the interests government adjusted and served as a massive agency for social control over most of the lives of most members of society.

New techniques in government, in the operations of interest groups and in the conduct of economic actors, render the separate as well as the coordinating controls ineffective. There are no effective compromises; there is no legitimacy; there is a 'crisis of justice'; the economic mechanisms do not work. The coordination of the new techniques so that they no longer act destructively requires planning. This can only be effective if controlled at the centre, although the plan can and should provide for a good deal of decentralization, planfully devolving planning functions to local authorities or some governmental agencies.

The new order which is needed can retain democratic procedures and parliamentary forms for legitimating decisions, and it should certainly do so, if political structures and traditions remain more or less intact. The old forms must, however, be filled with new contents. Mannheim defines 'politics', in the specific sense in which it refers to a type of social technique and not to the generic complex of all social control, as 'the struggle between the rival groups and authorities which determines the trend of development';[28] and he insists that 'the reduction of the political element is essential for any form of planning'.[29] Where controls are rationally coordinated, the control of controls must sooner or later be run on rationalized lines. Since it is the notion of class struggle which does most to exacerbate a politics of struggle, pacification achieved by wartime collaboration will have to be extended by a policy of economic welfare and equalization. In any case, 'elections may well be regarded as a guide only, as an ultimate indication to the consulting bodies who have to carry out the public's wishes'.[30] Mannheim is not very forthcoming on the characteristics of democracy, except for the continuation of old rituals and forms and a general notion of openness to merit. The term seems mostly to have an historical referent for him.

He does have more analytical things to say about the way in which governing is to control controls after the abandonment of liberal parliamentary emphases on compromise and law, as well as dependence on processes out of government control. His search for models leads to the effective though overly rigid techniques pioneered by absolutist armies, the brilliant psychological methods of 'Americanization' pervading the scheme of civic education in the United States, and the advanced coordination of all social forces under the control of totalitarian regimes.

Planning in the most intact liberal communities will make extensive use of 'indirect' techniques of control, using the new insights into the social psychological mechanisms at work to manipulate the settings which control human beings most effectively. Mannheim distinguishes a number of agencies of indirect control, including communities, associations, politics, fields, and situations, acknowledging that these are concepts derived from diverse disciplinary contexts, and not elements in an integral conceptual scheme.

Citing Durkheim as precursor, he pays special attention to fields and situations as especially illustrative of the subtle methods of integration required for complex societies. 'Field' structures constitute a 'world' within which conduct is controlled by 'social and natural laws' but directed to the ends intended by those who can regulate the norms defining the world. To act intelligibly in that world requires orientation to those norms, no matter what the psychological motives may be that impel the actor. 'Situations' are now defined more restrictively than in the rest of Mannheim's writings, although the specification sheds light on the wider uses as well. They are constraining contexts, like 'fields', but they are concrete and structured by factual interactions rather than by norms. They lend themselves, Mannheim says, to 'specific reconstruction and sociological readjustments' of the sort undertaken by social workers. Mannheim builds on the experiences of the educators and social workers so important in his new audience, but looks for ways of coordinating the mechanisms they employ.

'The ideal at which modern society is aiming', according to Mannheim, is to reinstate by design the situation which prevails by 'intuitive consent' in customary society, a regulation which is both 'totalitarian' and 'democratic'.[31] What Mannheim means, however, is a situation in which such basic values as cooperation and responsibility are so effectively inculcated that they can function as a reliable and unconstrained constitutional foundation upon which decision and action can rest. Since he is convinced that such values have been effectively destroyed by the mass, functioning as a power-ful reductionist control agency, he thinks that 'field' and 'situation' control, along with other techniques for mass-education, will have to restore that foundation. Mannheim speaks of 'articulating the mass', but acknowledges the important part he wants to assign to emotion-alism and the manipulation of mass ecstasy. The objective of the emotionalism is to create the security and constitutional value-order which will free individuals or, more likely, articulated groups from the mass and allow them to be rational.[32]

Mannheim contends that such coordinated 'totalitarian' con-trol is not antithetical to freedom in its modern sense. Planning will secure large areas of social space within which spontaneity will be given free play and no one will try to dictate the preferences of individuals among the choices available. The range of choices is always limited by the norms of the field concerned. Planning will make adjustments in norms by manipulating the relevant mechan-isms, but in this it will not differ in kind from earlier constitutions of 'freedom'. 'Freedom' in this sense contributes to the flexibility and ingenuity needed to solve old problems and meet new situations, especially among the elite. And 'freedom' in this sense provides a harmless or beneficial outlet for irrational drives, especially among the masses. In a surprising application of his earlier post-Hegelian vocabulary, he speaks of this as 'mastering the irrational'. Instances of such mastering, in this puzzling anticlimax, include the uses of sports in modern society, and the uses of advertising to prevent the 'chaos of consumer freedom', while allowing preferences free play.

Mannheim also uses these unpersuasive examples to support the contention that the regimen of total social control is by no means 'dehumanizing'. He thinks, quite to the contrary, that such provi-sions make life more 'natural' and less subject to instinctual repres-sion, while preserving the security of modern civil existence. In the same connection, Mannheim notes that control by means of situa-tions keeps the planners close to the 'creative tendencies in living material', and thus open to change, since controllers in touch with situations will sense that actions which are in violation of norms established in wider, more formal contexts, may be appropriate and positive responses to situations. Overall, Mannheim takes the social worker, like the psychoanalyst, as model for the capacity of modern social control techniques to give due recognition to emotion. With-out trying to rationalize all conduct, such controllers retain the dis-tance and detachment required for therapeutic intervention.

Although much of this may read like the textbook from which

Herbert Marcuse, a generation later, conned his model for 'repressive tolerance', Mannheim himself tries to address the issues which trouble Marcuse. He acknowledges that his whole political sociology sets forth a 'functional approach' embodying technical thinking. And he rehearses briefly but forcefully what he here calls 'romantic' objections to this sort of thinking. Now he is more inclined to say, at the general methodological level, that the objections are 'valid' and 'justified' but that they can nevertheless not be heeded because the rise in technical knowledge simply cannot be averted once the techniques are in effect, and because the process is already too far advanced for such scruples:

> Once the preliminary steps have been taken, we cannot escape the task of requiring sufficient technical skill to steer the social machine instead of letting ourselves be crushed beneath its wheels.[33]

The other time Mannheim had used this image was at the conclusion of 'Politics as a Science', when it was the 'party machine' that was flattening all before it. That time, however, he called for resistance at the last moment. Ten years had changed his attitude towards such machines.

But the fact that Mannheim places himself, as master of social technique, alongside of others who possess an antithetical vision which is also 'valid' and 'justified' is not merely nostalgia. He is also thinking about his relationship to the Moot. In the essay on 'Social Philosophy', which he prepared for the Moot,[34] Mannheim argues that Christian metaphysical thinking is a valuable complement to his own efforts. To perceive concrete, ultimately meaning-giving archetypes of human experience at the deepest level, he maintains, provides a dramatization of existence, which is essential to the constitution of commitment and action. While the theory of social control can neither generate nor test such truths, it must acknowledge that its own composition depends on some such ground of energy. Similarly, in an echo of a different earlier theme, Mannheim maintains that a genuine experience of 'presentness' presupposes a utopian projection of some sort, although a sociological theory cannot but undermine utopianism. What had earlier appeared as anomalies or contradictions requiring reflective theoretical treatment, if only in experimental essays, now provide mere tokens of depth in a theoretical texture which is not much troubled by them. The work remains at an uncritical level.

As a political theory, Mannheim's design has major flaws.

Mannheim fails to deal forthrightly with force and violence as aspects of political life or with coercion as an aspect of social control. A political theory which does not deal with the most signal political facts, a political history which leaps over the formative period of the modern state and moves from a stereotyped medievalism to a stereotyped liberalism, a conception of government that is wholly uninformative about its form or processes – such a conception of social control is one sided, ambiguous, undeveloped. There are suggestions, insights, reformulations and recombinations of earlier ideas, and there is an admirable display of great energy in taking the planning theme out of the repertory of the progressive thinking initiated before the First World War, and elaborating it into a comprehensive ideal type. In this capacity, the one-sided abstraction from the complexity of power relations is not a defect. By suggesting this wider context, Mannheim stimulated new thinking in such fields as education, social work, and economic planning. While he did not produce a new political theory, as he had hoped to do, he generated a useful model to identify new problems and possibilities.

NOTES

[1] Letter to Wirth, 13th August 1938.
[2] Letter to Wirth, 6th April 1939.
[3] Letter to Wirth, 17th September 1939.
[4] F. A. Iremonger, *William Temple, Archbishop of Canterbury* (London: Oxford University Press, 1948), p. 409.
[5] 'Some Remarks on *Humanisme Integral* by Jacques Maritain'. Two-page mimeograph, circulated to 'Moot' members prior to a dinner meeting with Maritain on May 11, 1939. The minutes and circulated letters of the 'Moot' are in the care of the Audenshaw foundation (Mucker, Richmond, England). Here quoted after L. Charles Cooper, *The Hindu Prince: A Sociological Biography of Karl Mannheim*, Vol. II: Appendices, unpublished typescript, pp. 148ff.
[6] Karl Mannheim to Oldham. Two-page 'Moot' mimeograph, circulated to 'Moot' members prior to their April 1941 meeting in Cold Ash, England. In Cooper, *loc. cit.*, pp. 190–191.
[7] *Ibid.*, p. 191.
[8] 'Some Remarks on *Humanisme Integral* by Jacques Maritain', p. 149.
[9] *Ibid.*

[10]   *The Times*, 11th January 1947, p. 7.

[11]   Roger Kojecky, *T. S. Eliot's Social Criticism* (New York: Farrar, Straus and Giroux, 1972), p. 155. This account of Mannheim and the Moot draws throughout on Kojecky's valuable work in the sources.

[12]   Michael Polanyi to Mannheim, 19th April 1944, University of Chicago, Joseph Regenstein Library, Archives.

[13]   Mannheim to Polanyi, 26th April 1944.

[14]   Polanyi to Mannheim, 2nd May 1944.

[15]   *'Sacrifice quotidien'* refers to the way in which Lukács is said to have characterized his conversion to Bolshevism. See David Kettler, 'Culture and Revolution: Lukács in the Hungarian Revolution of 1918/19', *Telos*, **10** (Winter 1971), p. 76.

[16]   Roger Kojecky, *T. S. Eliot's Social Criticism*.

[17]   *Ibid.*, pp. 175f.

[18]   'The Place of the Study of Modern Society in a Militant Democracy: Some Practical Suggestions', 10-page undated manuscript, probably written in May 1940. Archives of the University of Keele, Papers of Lord Lindsay of Birker (A. D. Lindsay).

[19]   *Ibid.*

[20]   'Topics for the next meeting of the Moot', eight-page 'Moot' mimeograph. In Cooper, *loc. cit.*, p. 165.

[21]   *Ibid.*, p. 168f.

[22]   'Topics for the next meeting of the Moot', in Cooper, *loc. cit.*, p. 169f.

[23]   *Ibid.*, p. 167.

[24]   'Letter from Karl Mannheim to Oldham', *ibid.*, pp. 224ff.

[25]   Kojecky, *op. cit.*, p. 174.

[26]   *Man and Society in an Age of Reconstruction* (London: Routledge & Kegan Paul, 1940), p. 270.

[27]   *Ibid.*, p. 247.

[28]   *Ibid.*, p. 294.

[29]   *Ibid.*, p. 360.

[30]   *Ibid.*

[31]   *Ibid.*, p. 328.

[32]   See also 'Mass Education and Group Analysis', in *Diagnosis of our Time* (London: Routledge & Kegan Paul, 1943).

[33]   *Man and Society*, p. 242.

[34]   'Toward a New Social Philosophy', chapter seven of *Diagnosis of Our Time*.

Conclusion: Sociology as a Vocation

In the 'Introduction' to *Man and Society*, Mannheim draws a firm distinction between scientific syntheses based on detailed sociological knowledge, like that which he himself sought to develop, and the kinds of syntheses projected by 'laymen':

> We must try to create a period of theoretical integration, an integration that must be carried out with the same sense of responsibility which the specialists always feel in approaching their particular problems. . . . [In the absence of this] the solution of [the most] vital questions fell into the hands of political dogmatists and literary essayists, who . . . rarely have had the benefit of the tradition and training that is needed for the responsible elaboration of scientific facts. . . . The literary essayist tries to achieve a kind of private synthesis, the key to which lies in the chance biographies of individual writers, rather than in the evidence of scientifically studied materials.[1]

This passage poses a special challenge to the present interpretation of Mannheim's achievement, since the approach interweaves a good deal of biographical information into the account, especially in treating his work in England, and repeatedly calls attention to Mannheim's dependence on the methods of the literary essayist. Justice to Mannheim requires a less polemical and less polarized understanding of the relationship between scientific and literary dimensions of intellectual production than he offers here, and it requires appreciation of the ways in which an open intellectual system like Mannheim's accommodates to the demands of the environment which it perceives. Self-clarification and diagnostic clarification of the environing 'times' are formative principles of Mannheim's scientific approach. And the findings of such study, in his view, always serve as symptoms of the situation, as well as diagnoses, provided the enquiries are conducted in a 'responsible' way.

It would be hard to substantiate the claim that Mannheim's experiments in theoretical integration achieved scientific thoroughness in their command of the detailed material or rigour in formulation. There are valuable reflections on sociological materials, like the essays on generations and on ambition in economic life, and powerful suggestions concerning sociological themes, especially in his work on sociology of knowledge. But the integrative designs retain the marks of their philosophical and literary provenance. The notion of sociology of knowledge as an 'organon for politics as a science', for example, depends on conceptions of theoretical grounding and historical development for which no adequate sociological warrant is offered. Yet the result is a fascinating projection of the ideological process and of its possible transformation. In this case, the ingenious essayistic response to a constellation in the political situation yields insights and stimulus to more systematic investigation. The overly dramatized *topos* of 'crisis' in the later work, in contrast, inclines him towards forced simplifications, like the stylized confrontations between 'mass' and 'elite', even while it gives vigour to his diagnostic writings. Both themes serve to integrate Mannheim's social thought, at different times, yet both are importantly products of Mannheim's sense of his 'mission' or 'vocation'.

His conjunction of 'responsibility' with the work of 'specialists' recalls his preoccupation with Max Weber's distinction between the vocations of politics and science, and implicitly reasserts the demand for synthesis between them. The political scientist who is also a scientific politician is to display responsibility with regard to the facts of his situation, reflexive as well as external. And that may require him to adopt a mode of rationality which does not accord with the norms of scientific work free of such responsibilities, a mode which is sensitive to problems of rhetorical effectiveness beyond the problems of communication alone.

If the choice of action depends on the ways in which individuals locate themselves within their situations and not simply on the selection of means adequate to the ends preferred, practical knowledge competent to guide choice must have the force to make those whom it addresses reconsider their own identities. That is another formulation of the ancient Socratic injunction to self-examination, and it implies, as Plato saw, a complex therapeutic encounter between the teacher and the taught. Both must expose themselves in the character formed by the 'chance biography' of each, but they must structure their encounter so as to lead to a common knowledge, made possible by the new situation they have jointly created.

Jürgen Habermas is perhaps the writer of the present generation who has most conscientiously attempted to build a theory of enlightenment upon such considerations. While the project of pursuing such knowledge is highly controversial, the recognition that practical knowledge, say in the form of 'social policy analysis' must have a structure and logic different from scientific knowledge as such, is gaining new empirical support.[2] Mannheim's sociological accomplishments, in any case, must be understood within the context of his efforts to work on both of these problems. His own attention to his situation, the conditions determining his communication with a revelant public as well as the larger historical setting, was integral to his theoretical strategy. It is a tragic feature of his story that these considerations drew him ever more towards formulations which rendered his own project obscure, as witness the distinction between 'laymen' and 'specialists' in the discussion cited above, and the very notion of 'thought at the level of planning' to which it refers. His most original and brilliant contribution is the suggestion that 'ideologies' may approximate to the structures of practical social knowledge by virtue of the very features which make them radically inadequate as scientific theories and which make them comprehensible only in the context of their social functions. His later retreat from that suggestion makes sense in the light of the intrinsic difficulties arising out of the proposal and the demands made on him by his project and by the changed circumstances of his life.

Relating Mannheim to the situations and audiences he addresses, accordingly, is not in any way meant to reduce his work to an artifact of his personal biography or, absurdly, to class Mannheim with those he calls 'laymen'. His was a life in and for sociology in a deeply instructive sense. He was a profoundly creative sociologist, and, as Jean Floud has observed, one of the last of the 'major figures' in the discipline, recognized as representative and authoritative within and without the community of professional social scientists. His best essays interrogate the discipline as much as they utilize the discipline to interrogate the social world. His great and constitutive question was whether sociology can provide the integral and comprehensive practical knowledge which liberalism requires in order to master the disruptive irrationalities first projected by the critics of liberalism and then brutally real in the events of the twentieth century. His tragedy as a thinker was that in his mature years he was forced to pursue his enquiry under conditions which made much of what he had accomplished before appear irrelevant and useless to him.

Many of those Mannheim sought to address in England and America could not understand his theoretical interest at all, taking his systematizing statements as manifestations of a continental weakness for abstruse speculation. Others carried on their own theoretical discourse in modalities to which Mannheim was largely tone-deaf, and they avenged his seeming indifference to their accomplishments by their response to his efforts. The one group, exemplified by the Moot, humoured his weakness for system-building, but were satisfied to abstract the many 'ideas' they found rewarding. The other, including some of his professional colleagues, finally 'reacted furiously to him. . . . and considered him a charlatan who confused young people' by posing 'deep' but unanswerable questions 'but couldn't teach them anything because he didn't have anything valuable to teach'.[3] Both kinds of responses worked back on Mannheim's theoretical efforts, to their marked detriment.

Mannheim was sincerely respected and admired by a number of people of real intellectual achievement during his years on the Moot. They secured him the position at the Institute of Education and they helped him to found the International Library of Sociology and Social Reconstruction at Routledge & Kegan Paul. And they publicly thanked him for suggestions and praised him for his ideas. But they did not take his theories seriously, as he wanted them taken. His admirers on the Moot – A. D. Lindsay, Fred Clarke, T. S. Eliot – agreed with his general political search for a form of planning as compatible as possible with established values and institutions, and they were stimulated by his ideas.

But the distinctly English sense of 'ideas', as separately reasoned opinions on discrete questions, stands opposed to Mannheim's lifelong search for philosophically grounded structures of knowledge and, indeed, to John Stuart Mill's aspirations in the *Logic of the Moral Sciences*.[4] A. D. Lindsay, for example, closed a review of Mannheim's posthumous *Freedom, Power and Democratic Planning* with the wish that 'someone could write a short and popular book called "The Wisdom of Mannheim" which might be widely read'. This 'wisdom' does not depend on Mannheim's conception of sociological theory as synthetical knowledge.

> Doctor Mannheim knows so much, has such a proper consciousness of the altogetherness of everything, and the way in which any one factor in society may affect others, that it is very difficult for him to leave things alone. I remember discussing with him and a group of friends containing H. H. Oldham how social reform ought best to come about, and I maintained that you must make up your mind as to what in society was of the most danger, and grapple with that, and assume that modern society was naturally healthy, and would somehow deal with other things that are rotten. Mannheim stoutly maintained that you could do nothing until you knew exactly what to do for everything ... Mannheim always resisted very strongly any suggestion that legislation, like moral action, was partly a leap in the dark. One always felt that he had a sociological faith that all these blanks of ignorance about society could be overcome.[5]

As interesting as the good-natured scepticism about Mannheim's theoretical design is the recurrent turn to the biographical, in this as in similar reviews of his later achievements. Mannheim had become a prominent personality – forceful, interesting, articulate – a figure in cultural and intellectual life, a lively and stimulating conversationalist.

That personality was not everywhere appreciated. One younger contemporary has recalled:

> There was something in his conversational manner that appeared 'slippery'. He trimmed and adjusted what he was saying, in order to forestall objections and keep the flow. He sought thereby to create the impression of general agreement, even when his evasions left the point quite muddled and his partner in conversation often quite frustrated. What might have seemed fair to him appeared opportunistic and more pre-emptive than accommodating to others.[6]

But much other testimony, like that of T. S. Eliot, emphasizes Mannheim's brilliance. In his supplement to the *Times* obituary, Eliot said:

> In informal discussion among a small group, he gained an ascendancy which he never sought, but which was, on the contrary, imposed upon him by the eagerness of others to listen to what he had to say. . . . His talk was always a stimulant to original thought.[7]

It is quite in keeping with this high opinion, however, that Eliot took the lead among those resisting Mannheim's attempts to unify the Moot in doctrine and action. For Eliot, the purpose of conversation is to study types, to seek knowledge about things, to get responses, to be stimulated. In a Moot paper, Eliot wrote:

> It is not the business of clerics to agree with each other; they are driven to each other's company by their common dissimilarity from everybody else, and by the fact that they find each other the most profitable people to disagree with.[8]

This conception is far removed from Mannheim's hopes for an organization of intellectuals for common tasks of policy guidance and popularization.

Another feature of the exchange of ideas which the English milieu cultivated and Mannheim sought in vain to coordinate is the ease with which one attractive idea is replaced by another. When A. D. Lindsay began planning the university that became Keele, for example, 'Mannheim was one of the first people he wanted to consult. . . . He was very much impressed by Mannheim's stress on sociology and social awareness'.[9] On a subsequent occasion, however, he was struck by a remark by his wife that 'we in England . . . get our *Weltanschauung* from . . . poetry'.[10] The latter conception had more to do with the design of Keele's curriculum, and it was 1966 before there was a full Professor of Sociology appointed at Keele.

Similarly, Fred Clarke opened his influential book on *Education and Social Change* with a summary of Mannheim's thesis about the transition to planning and especially about the need to overcome the lack of self-awareness about ideology in English thinking, as well as the inability to work through comprehensive designs. But a year or two later, at a LePlay House Conference, Clarke rejected the idea of sociology in the school curriculum and pleaded for history, quoting

R. G. Collingwood, 'The idea of action as duty . . . is inevitable to a person who considers it historically'.[11] Even Mannheim's most ardent supporters, in short, distanced themselves from his style of thought.

There were successes and major achievements in the programme of publications he initiated at Routledge & Kegan Paul. He attempted to foster an international community of intellectuals which – as in Hungary and Germany and the earlier years in England – he saw as being already everywhere at work. He made special efforts to naturalize some of the intellectual currents which had influenced his own earlier development, including a book on Dilthey by Moot associate, publications by Lukács, and writings by German existentialist writers who had not emigrated. Despite the recognition involved in that work, however, an exchange of letters between his two closest collaborators documents the pattern of misunderstanding and non-reciprocity which haunts his later endeavours. There is an unpleasant undercurrent of shared assumptions in the brief correspondence between Lindsay, one of the four prestigious members of the Library's Advisory Board, and T. Murray Ragg, the responsible official at the publishing company. Lindsay writes about the manuscript of the book on Dilthey:

> I think it would be a much better book to publish than some of the stuff you have got in the library, but then I think the library is a mixture of very good stuff and some books the only justification for which was that they were written by distressed Germans. But Mannheim never consulted anyone.

Ragg replied:

> Your comment about books in the library interested me very much, and perhaps you will have some sympathy with me when I tell you that for every book accepted by us for the library at Mannheim's urgent request, we turned down at least a dozen equally urgently put before us. It was difficult indeed to keep him on any sort of leash. We are now, however, trying to maintain a much higher standard, though there are still many legacies from the Mannheim regime to appear.[12]

The question of Mannheim's relations with his special audience is important to an understanding of his thought, because he himself made the element of connection with a collective consciousness a constitutive element of his experimental theoretical structures. A crucial part of the experiment for him was the testing of resonance. In a sense, the conception is congruent with Lukács's conception of class-consciousness, but the experience of connectedness and inter-subjective grounding was to be more empirical in character: not the elucidation of objective interests and tendencies alone, but the acknowledged clarification of the practices actuating the real unit – a generation, an intelligentsia, a discipline, a spiritual elite – rendering it fully actual and articulate. Mannheim's attempts to achieve such results were jeopardized by actual resistance in the groups addressed, who often did not recognize themselves in his account of them, and by some tendency towards self-deception, strengthened by the sheer energy with which he embarked on his efforts and the frustration in finding his means insufficient, intensified in the resistant new cultural context. Without producing the experience of 'insight' in the 'patient' – to adapt Mannheim's favourite analogy – the diagnosis was 'not valid' and the 'therapy' without effect.

Much has been written about the contributions which the immigrant scholars made to the cultural and social sciences in England and North America, and rightly so. But perhaps not enough has been said about the costs of that emigration to the scholars. They found themselves forced to choose between accepting a role as alien and esoteric prophets, praised for the 'heuristic' value of their work for the ongoing scholarly enterprise but not as contributors to the going concern, or recasting their thought into modes whose capacities for subtlety they could not easily master. A witness well qualified to speak, who opted for each of these alternatives in turn, wrote at the time:

> Every émigré intellectual, without exception, is damaged. And he better admit it, if he does not want to have the harsh lesson brought home to him behind the tightly closed doors of his self-esteem. He lives in surroundings that must remain incomprehensible to him, however well he may find his way among labor organizations or in traffic. He constantly dwells in confusion. . . . His language has been expropriated, and the historical dimension, that nourished his knowledge, has been sapped.[3]

While the intellectual communities in the host countries could often make productive use of the stimulation they received, this usefulness was not necessarily good for the refugees and for their own further intellectual development. The loss of a language rich with meanings and the loss of an audience responsive to that language may indeed sometimes work as stimulus to new creativity. But it will more commonly work harm. The author may attempt to translate his thoughts into an idiom whose conceptual apparatus will not easily bear it and which he does not fully command. Or he may coin new formulations to do the job in the new language, but they are likely to be still-born, dead words in a ritualized vocabulary, reified and stylized as they are expounded and defended, and antithetical to the movement of thought. Mannheim's theorizing was victimized in this way, despite the fact that his earlier work on the context-dependency of concepts in the cultural sciences uniquely prepared him for the problems he faced.

He felt obliged to make a rapid contribution, to repay his reception as a refugee and to earn his due place. Accordingly, he did not follow the advice which he himself had given Wirth in 1930, to live 'there' for a while in order to see how 'scientific problems' are posed from 'within the immediate problem context there'. His turn to John Stuart Mill, in an initial accommodation to Ginsberg, was well-conceived; but he used it more as an opening to Saint-Simon and Comte than as a starting point for exploring the British line of social enquiry, back from Mill, through Stewart and Millar to Ferguson and Smith, and forward from Mill, to Geddes and Hobhouse. As a result, he sometimes appeared arrogant and ill-informed to important colleagues, and lost important opportunities. Mannheim himself, it should be recalled, professed to find that the condition of being a refugee provided a position of strategic marginality and a unique capacity for intermediation. He hoped to 'serve as a living interpreter between different cultures and to create living communications between different worlds which so far have been kept apart'.[14] But he underestimated the liabilities of this emigration.

Throughout all his work, Mannheim maintained that there was such a thing as a 'spirit of the age' to be uncovered, that he could bring that spirit to the consciousness of those he was addressing, and that communion with that spirit would provide knowledge that is both valid and efficacious. As was the case with the young John Stuart Mill, who also found the notion of a spirit of the age inspiring, the conception led him to a search for possible grounds of consensus among the best minds of the age, and for ways of expanding the influence of those who had been thus brought to agreement. The practical side of this resembles the attitude and design of a politician, but the premises embody a conception of non-conflictual politics which has no room for politicians. A Ciceronian statesman is required, and this sets in motion the classical humanist vicious circle, in that such statesmanship presupposes the recognition for which it is supposed to lay the foundation.[15]

Mannheim's search for the spirit, the synthesis, the consensus he thought to be incipiently emerging, produced a handsome, non-sectarian openness towards ideas from many sources. But it also led to insistence that there is 'something more' to each of them, so that the conflicting demands for adherence from the various intellectual sources consulted did not have to be seriously entertained. The appearance of emerging consensus is given by a 'slippery' relationship to other minds: curious, engaged, responsive, but never taking them on their terms. He would locate their thoughts within a schematized development, or subject key concepts to a 'change of function'. It was unnecessary to criticize what others said; it was enough to correct and balance it, by drawing on something said by someone else. All were seen to be manifesting symptoms of the same condition or expressing the same spirit.

In Central Europe, the spirit had something to do, in the last analysis, with the *logos* of German Humanism, vaguely apprehended by the diverse Idealist philosophies but needing to be made social flesh. In England, it was the underlying ethos of the gentleman which could revive democracy, leadership, and responsible control, restoring health after the smouldering crisis. The gentlemanly ethos would have to be sublimated, so as to be less bound by time and place, but it already combined in itself practical responsibility and mental cultivation, Mannheim thought, and this combination was the key to substantive rationality. Much of this rested on illusion. Mannheim's dependence on those who shared these illusions weakened his critical insight and, especially in the English setting, diminished his capacity for the irony and self-reflection which is required to balance such earnestness.

In Germany, Mannheim spoke a language with resonant cultural appeal: his audiences filled in meanings and found that his ambiguities stimulated them to think about their own uncertainties. The essay form which he used encouraged him to allow for the complementarity of diverse approaches and fostered reflection on that diversity. At times, as in *Conservatism*, these reflections experimented with such designs as Müller's bipolar dialectic, mediating between opposites without claiming to have reintegrated them within a transcendent third term. At other times, Mannheim considered pluralistic philosophical alternatives. But throughout, he treated the human world of thinking and acting as superior to his intellectual constructs. He sought for knowledge to inform creative action, not to take its place. Using the idiom of sociology, he achieved results like those of the great literary essayists of his time. If he had not been expelled from Germany, he might have turned to good use the substantial responses and criticisms he was getting from people of his own generation like Hannah Arendt, Norbert Elias, Max Horkheimer, Herbert Marcuse, Hans Speier, and Paul Tillich.[16] His work might have become more rigorous, as philosophy or history or sociology, or it might have attained greater power and forthrightness while remaining within the genres of critical essay and commentary. But the English adjustment exacted great costs. He was bound to be misunderstood, and to feel himself misunderstood.

His persistence was marvellous, his determination to be heard and to be accepted as a guide. In the 'Preliminary Approach' to *Ideology and Utopia*, he offers the parallel with Socrates; and then there is the 'mission of the refugee', the Sociologist in the *Summa* of the Moot, the summoner to international reconstruction. Yet in addition to the influential writings and the influenced people, there are also appalling misunderstandings. Mannheim's achievements would do honour to any thinker about society. The vagaries of his thinking matter only because his sociological accomplishments are so important. The flaws appear great and had bad effects on the direction of the work itself because of Mannheim's aspirations and his conception of what he was about. Mannheim presents a dilemma to the sociological profession, unfinished business, in the way that Hegel, Marx and Weber were unfinished business for Mannheim. Yet in the present unsettled state of the discipline, where recent divisions into static 'camps' appear ever more outdated, there may be a new capacity for recognizing in Mannheim not only a key innovator in sociological enquiry but also a representative figure whose difficulties cannot be smoothed out by interpretation. They can only be addressed by taking up the work of critical self-reflection where he was deflected from it.

NOTES

[1]   *Man and Society in an Age of Reconstruction* (London: Routledge & Kegan Paul, 1940), p. 31.

[2]   Cf. Mark van de Vall and Cheryl A. Bolas, 'External vs.

Internal Policy Researchers', *Knowledge: Creation, Diffusion, Utilization,* **2,** 4 (June 1981); Mark van der Vall and Cheryl A. Bolas, 'Using Social Policy Research for Reducing Social Problems', *The Journal of Applied Behavioral Science,* **18,** 1 (1982).

[3]   Personal Interview with Jean Floud, March 2, 1976.

[4]   Cf. Robert D. Cumming, 'Is Man Still Man?', *Social Research,* **40,** 3 (1973) pp. 481–510.

[5]   Lord Lindsay of Birker in *British Journal of Sociology,* **3,** pp. 85–86 (1952).

[6]   Personal Interview with Jean Floud (March 2, 1976). Mrs Floud has written extremely well on Mannheim and has been the only commentator to notice the importance of Jaszi to Mannheim. As Jean McDonald, she worked with him on the revision of *Ideology and Utopia* and joined him for a summer of work in Budapest in the late 1930s, where he and his wife used to spend many holidays. See for example, Jean Floud, 'Karl Mannheim (1893–1947)' in A. V. Judges, ed., *The Function of Teaching* (London, 1959).

[7]   T. S. Eliot, 'Professor Karl Mannheim', *The Times,* 25 January 1947, p. 7.

[8]   T. S. Eliot, 'On the Place and Function of the Clerisy', circulated to Moot members in November, 1944, in Cooper, *The Hindu Prince: A Sociological Biography of Karl Mannheim,* unpublished typescript, p. 233.

[9]   Drusilla Scott, *A. D. Lindsay, A Biography* (Oxford: Basil Blackwell, 1971), p. 344.

[10] Sir James Mountford, *Keele: An Historical Critique* (London: Routledge & Kegan Paul, 1972), p. 370.

[11] Dorothy M. E. Dymes, ed., *Sociology and Education* (Malvern: LePlay House Press, 1944), p. 95.

[12] Routledge & Kegan Paul files.

[13] Theodor Adorno, *Minima Moralia* (Frankfurt am Main: Suhrkamp, [1951]1969), p. 32.

[14] Karl Mannheim, 'The Function of the Refugee', *The New English Weekly,* **27,** 1 (April 19, 1945).

[15] On this see Robert Denoon Cumming, *Human Nature and History* (Chicago and London: University of Chicago Press, 1969), Vol. 1, pp. 203ff.

[16] See their contributions to the sociology of knowledge dispute in Weimar Germany, in Volker Meja and Nico Stehr, eds,

Der Streit um die Wissenssoziologie (Frankfurt Suhrkamp, 1982).
Also in the forthcoming English edition, *The Sociology of the Knowledge Dispute* (London: Routledge & Kegan Paul, 1984).

Suggestions for Further Reading

Readers unfamiliar with Mannheim's work are advised to begin with Kurt H. Wolff's *From Karl Mannheim* (London: Oxford University Press, 1971), which, in addition to a helpful introduction, contains several important essays by Mannheim (including 'The Problem of a Sociology of Knowledge', 'Conservative Thought', and 'Competition as a Cultural Phenomenon'). Mannheim's best-known work is *Ideology and Utopia* (London: Routledge & Kegan Paul, 1936), which a serious reader should take on next. But in view of the findings reported in the present book – that in the English edition there is a shift from the theoretical frame influenced by Marxism, historicism, and Idealism, toward empiricism, psychologism, and pragmatism – the German original *Ideologie und Utopie*, 3rd edn, (Frankfurt: Schulte-Bulmke, 1952) should also be consulted wherever possible.

Other important works by Mannheim include *Man and Society in an Age of Reconstruction* (London: Routledge & Kegan Paul, 1940), *Diagnosis of Our Time* (London: Routledge & Kegan Paul, 1943), and a number of the posthumously published collections of Mannheim's essays, which should be consulted with the awareness that most of the texts were not prepared for publication by Mannheim himself, and that the available versions reflect a variety of editorial policies. These collections include: *Freedom, Power and Democratic Planning*

(London: Routledge & Kegan Paul, 1950); *Essays on the Sociology of Knowledge* (London: Routledge & Kegan Paul, 1952); *Essays on Sociology and Social Psychology* (London: Routledge & Kegan Paul, 1953); *Essays on the Sociology of Culture* (London: Routledge & Kegan Paul, 1956); *Structures of Thinking* (London: Routledge & Kegan Paul, 1982); and the forthcoming *Conservatism* (London: Routledge & Kegan Paul, 1985).

There is a considerable amount of secondary literature on Mannheim, mostly in essay form. The most sympathetic book is A. P. Simonds's *Karl Mannheim's Sociology of Knowledge* (Oxford: Clarendon Press, 1978), which we highly recommend. Kurt H. Wolff's introduction to *From Karl Mannheim* is also excellent. Other useful secondary literature, written from various theoretical perspectives, includes: Robert K. Merton's and C. Wright Mills's pioneering essays on Mannheim and the sociology of knowledge in *Social Theory and Social Structure*, revised edn. (Glencoe: Free Press of Glencoe, 1957) and *Power, Politics and People*, ed. I. L. Horowitz (New York: Ballantine, 1963); Karl Popper's *The Poverty of Historicism* (London: Routledge & Kegan Paul, 1961); J. J. Macquet's *The Sociology of Knowledge: Its Structure and its Relation to the Philosophy of Knowledge* (Boston: Beacon Press, 1951); Werner Stark's *The Sociology of Knowledge: An Essay in Aid of a Deeper Understanding of the History of Ideas* (London: Routledge & Kegan Paul, 1958); Nicholas Abercrombie's *Class, Structure and Knowledge* (Oxford: Blackwell, 1980); Peter Hamilton's *Knowledge and Social Structure* (London: Routledge & Kegan Paul, 1974); and Lewis Coser's chapter on Mannheim in his *Masters of Sociological Thought* (New York: Harcourt Brace, 1971). Gunter W. Remmling's *The Sociology of Karl Mannheim* (London: Routledge & Kegan Paul, 1975) is also useful, particularly in regard to the sociology of social planning, but the book is generally marred by an overly simple interpretation of Mannheim's work.

The Hungarian phase of Mannheim's work, which is treated only cursorily in the present book, is covered in David Kettler's 'Culture and Revolution', *Telos*, **10** (1971). The sociology of knowledge dispute in Germany, which was initiated by Mannheim's work in Weimar Germany, is discussed in a forthcoming anthology: Volker Meja and Nico Stehr, eds, *The Sociology of Knowledge Dispute* (London: Routledge & Kegan Paul, 1984).

The books by A. P. Simonds and Gunter Remmling contain excellent bibliographical guides through the secondary literature. Both of these books and the book by Wolff contain fairly complete bibliographies of Mannheim's work.

Index

A

Abercrombie, Nicholas, 165
Abrams, Philip, 128
Adorno, Theodor, 162
Aquinas, St. Thomas, 132
Summa theologiae, 132–3
Arendt, Hannah, 12, 30, 161

B

Balász, Béla, 38
Baldamus, W., 79
Bentham, Jeremy, 134
Bolas, Cheryl A., 160–1
Branford, Sybella Gurney, 120, 128
Branford, Victor, 119, 120, 128
Brinckmann, Carl, 42
Budapest, 11, 14, 18, 19, 38, 41, 134, 135
Burke, Kenneth, 78

C

Cassirer, Ernst, 107, 126
Cattell, Raymond B., 127
Cezanne, Paul, 77
Christianity and Christians, 131–7, 143, 148
Clarke, Sir Fred, 131, 154, 156
Cohen, J. I., 231

Coleridge, Samuel T., 134
Collingwood, R. G., 156
Communism and Communists, 37–9, 110, 133, 136, 142, 143
Comte, Auguste, 23, 89, 101, 103, 120–2, 138, 159
Congdon, Lee, 77
conservatism, 18, 26–7, 30, 42, 43–4, 54–5, 64–5, 94, 133
constitution, 67–8, 78, 146–7
Cooper, Charles, 125, 149, 150
Coser, Lewis, 165
crisis, 13, 15, 22, 36, 38, 59, 67, 74, 91–104, 112, 132, 137, 144, 152
Cumming, Robert Denoon, 21–3, 25–6, 31, 162
Curtius Ernst Robert, 108, 126

D

Dahl, Robert A., 12
Dawson, Christopher, 138
democracy, 19, 20, 22, 24, 66–8, 97–9, 104, 137, 145–6
Dewey, John, 12, 18, 80, 87
dialectics, 13, 45–6, 66–7, 70, 90, 97, 138, 160
Dilthey, Wilhelm, 59, 75, 157

Dostoyevsky, Fyodor, 36, 38, 39, 77
Dugdale, J. E., 128
Durkheim, Emile, 80, 81, 119, 122, 137, 146
Dymes, Dorothy M. E., 162

E

Eckehart, Meister, 38
economics, 19, 66, 71, 82–4
Elias, Norbert, 161
Eliot, T. S., 131, 139, 154, 156
elite, 81, 86, 89, 94, 97–8, 110, 121, 129, 138–40, 152, 158
Ellis, Havelock, 127
empiricism and empirical methods, 13, 23, 42, 44–5, 49, 70, 72, 74, 85, 113, 133, 135
enlightenment, 43–4, 76, 86–7, 90–1, 101, 153
epistemology, 11, 24–6, 37, 42, 48–52, 67, 70, 73
Ernst, Paul, 77
essay-writing, 13, 22, 34–5, 47–8, 71, 74–5, 94, 106, 113, 115–7, 127, 148, 151–2, 160

F

Farmer, Herbert H., 138
Farquharson, Alexander, 120
Fascism, 69, 73, 76, 83, 87, 110, 129, 133, 142
Ferguson, Adam, 159
Floud, Jean (Jean McDonald), 112, 128, 153, 162
Fraenkel, Ernst, 66
freedom, 21, 28, 44, 138, 147
Freud, Sigmund, 80–1
Freyer, Hans, 100
Fromm, Erich, 87

G

Gábor, Éva, 77
Gabel, Joseph, 127
Geddes, Sir Patrick, 119, 120, 159
generation, 13, 47, 55–6, 107, 109, 158
George, Stefan and Stefan-George-Circle, 38–40, 71
Gerth, Hans H., 79
Ginsberg, Morris, 109–11, 118–23, 128–9, 159
Goethe, Johann Wolfgang, 35–6

H

Habermas, Juergen, 153
Haldane, J. B. S., 127
Hamilton, Peter, 165
Hayek, Friedrich, 12
Hegel, Georg Wilhelm Friedrich, 17, 37–8, 42, 45, 57, 60, 64, 70, 114, 116, 147
Heidegger, Martin, 52
Heidelberg, 38–40
Hermann, Ulrich, 79
historicism, 26, 44–5, 70, 90, 103
history, 24, 26, 39, 44, 53, 57, 86, 90, 99–100, 103–5, 113, 124, 135–6
  philosophy of history, 34, 37, 41, 48, 53, 63, 70, 101
Hitler, Adolf, 93, 141
  Mein Kampf, 136
Hobhouse, Leonard, 111, 119, 120, 122, 159
Hobson, John A., 121
Hodges, H. A., 131
Horkheimer, Max, 12, 161
Horney, Karen, 87
Horowitz, Irving Louis, 165
Horváth, Zoltán, 31
Hugo, Gustav, 46
Husserl, Edmund, 52, 53

I

Idealism, 23, 35–7, 49, 53, 68, 160
ideology, 13, 26, 28, 34, 43, 52, 54–76, 103, 153
Ideology and Utopia, 12, 15, 28, 34, 47, 64–5, 116–7
  German and English versions compared, 27, 31–2, 78, 110–116
intellectuals and intelligentsia, 13, 15–6, 20, 28–30, 33, 39–40, 49, 54, 58–62, 68–70, 93, 96–7, 106, 109, 113, 115, 117–8, 133, 137, 156, 158
Iremonger, Frederick A., 149

J

Jászi, Oscar, 14, 18–25, 28, 31, 38, 95, 120, 134
Jews and Jewishness, 11, 14, 134, 142
Judges, Arthur V., 162

K

Kahler, Erich von, 71
Kant, Immanuel and (neo)-Kantianism, 23, 34, 38, 41, 49, 73, 115, 117, 135
Kecskemeti, Paul, 77, 126
Kelsen, Hans, 66–8, 78
Kierkegaard, Soeren Aabye, 38, 77
Kojecky, Roger, 150

L

Lask, Emil, 77
Laski, Harold, 11, 109, 111
law and legality, 15, 67–8, 99, 145–6
Lederer, Emil, 11, 42
Lenin, V. I., 59
LePlay, Frederic, 120
liberalism, 14, 18, 21–29, 39, 44, 46, 48, 55, 58, 60, 66, 71, 81, 89, 95–99, 100–1, 104, 110, 121, 133–4, 144, 149, 154
Lindblom, Charles E., 12
Lindsay, A. D. (Lord Lindsay of Birker), 131–2, 140, 154–7
Locke, John, 21
London School of Economics, 108, 110, 119, 130
Loewe, Adolph, 71–2, 81–2, 131
Lukacs, Georg, 14, 31, 35–9, 41, 46, 53, 59, 77, 103, 134, 136, 150, 157, 158
Luthardt, Wolfgang, 78

M

MacIver, Robert, 111
Macquet, J. J., 165
Malinowski, Bronislav, 127
Mann, Thomas, 25
Marcus-Tar, Judith, 31
Marcuse, Herbert, 12, 148, 161
Maritain, Jacques, 132–3
Marshall, Alfred, 122
Marshall, Thomas H., 120, 121, 123, 126, 128
Marx, Karl and Marxism, 24, 26, 38, 45–6, 53, 55, 58, 60–1, 64, 66, 69, 92, 100–1, 103, 111–2, 136–7, 144, 161
mass, 97–9, 137, 147, 152
McDougall, William, 127
Meinecke, Friedrich, 53
Merton, Robert K., 12, 165

method and methodology, 17, 22–3, 40–4, 46, 50–2, 55, 61–2, 70, 107, 124, 129, 148
Mill, John Stuart, 21–25, 28, 31, 88, 90, 101, 118, 121, 134, 154, 159
Millar, John, 159
Mills, C. Wright, 12, 165
Moberly, Sir Walter, 143–4
Moeser, Justus, 44
Moot, the, 129–132, 136–44, 148, 154, 156
Mountford, Sir James, 162
Mueller, Adam, 44–5, 160
Mumford, Louis, 12
Murry, John Middleton, 131–2
Myrdal, Gunnar, 65

N

National Socialism and Nazis, 11, 14, 75, 80, 84, 93, 136, 138, 142
Nisbet, Robert, 30

O

Oldham, J. H., 130–2, 138–44
ontology, 51–3, 72
Oppenheimer, Franz, 11, 71
organon, 40, 46, 48, 62, 70, 74, 86, 112, 114
Ortega Y Gasset, Jose, 80

P

Pareto, Vilfredo, 59
parliamentarism, 19, 27, 28, 99, 138, 145
phenomenology, 34, 64, 70, 72–3
plan and planning, 18, 19, 29, 35, 51, 71, 81–8, 100–1, 137, 145–9
Plato, 153
pluralism, 34, 37, 51, 67, 70, 160
Polanyi, Karl, 134
Polanyi, Michael, 134–6, 150
political education, 22–3, 28, 141
political theory, 15–6, 144, 148–9
politics and the political, 13, 15, 40, 48, 54, 59, 66, 81, 99–102, 115–6, 144, 159
Popper, Karl R., 12, 165
popularization, 25, 156
positivism, 17, 21, 34, 39, 49, 73, 89, 96, 118
psychoanalysis, 29, 80–1, 87–8, 147

R

Ragg, T. Murray, 157
reductionism, 37, 44, 52, 147
refugee, 15, 106, 108, 117, 134, 158–9
relativism, 22, 24, 37, 46–7, 52, 63, 69,
    73, 102, 118
Remmling, Gunter W., 165
revolution, 19, 38–9, 45, 67, 83, 92, 96,
    101, 103, 139, 141, 143
Rickert, Heinrich, 53
Riegl, Alois, 77
Robbins, Lionel, 126
Romanticism, 35–7, 40, 44, 49, 53, 69,
    90, 101, 148

S

Saage, Richard, 79
Saint-Simon, Henri de, 89, 103–4, 134,
    138, 159
Savigny, F. K. von, 44–7, 64
Scheler, Max, 30, 47–8, 53, 59
Schelting, Alexander von, 116, 117
science, 20, 22–7, 30, 37, 89, 106, 116,
    132, 135–6, 151
Scott, Drusilla, 162
Shils, Edward, 111–3, 127
Sidgwick, Henry, 122
Siebeck, Paul, 48
Simmel, Georg, 11, 59, 122
Simonds, Arthur P., 78, 165
situation, 13, 57, 83, 89, 93, 99, 101, 116,
    133, 142, 146, 152–3
Smith, Adam, 21, 82, 159
social techniques, 145–8
Socialism, 19, 20, 46, 54–5, 58, 73
sociology of knowledge, 12, 15–17, 29,
    42, 52–68, 110, 138, 152
Socrates, 113, 161
Sombart, Nicolaus, 103–4, 126
Spann, Othmar, 59
Speier, Hans, 117, 161
Spencer, Herbert, 21, 23

Spengler, Oswald, 71, 77, 79, 93
Stahl, F. J., 60
Stalin, Joseph, 59
Stark, Werner, 165
Stein, Lorenz von, 104
Stewart, Dugald, 159
style of thought, 18, 43–4, 56, 68
synthesis, 15, 26–30, 45–6, 60, 66, 76,
    101–2, 150

T

Temple, William, 131
Tillich, Paul, 12, 161
Toennies, Ferdinand, 78
totalitarianism, 94, 97, 99, 104, 131, 138,
    146
Travers, R. M. W., 127
Troeltsch, Ernst, 47, 53, 60, 71, 134

U

utopia, 74–5, 148

V

van der Wall, Mark, 161–2
Vierkandt, Alfred, 79, 111, 122

W

Weber, Alfred, 11, 39, 42, 60, 75, 80
Weber, Max, 17, 29, 38–9, 40, 42, 46–7,
    53–5, 59, 61, 64, 68, 70–72,
    80–1, 115, 118, 121, 137, 140,
    152, 161
Westermarck, Edward A., 122
Wilson, Charles H., 117–8
Wirth, Louis, 30, 108–9, 111–9, 129, 159
Wolff, Kurt H., 31, 77–8, 164–5
Wolin, Sheldon, 30

Z

Zalai, Béla, 77
Zimmern, Alfred E., 132